Two Decades of New Panchayati Raj in Karnataka

The Institute of Social Sciences

The Institute of Social Sciences was founded in 1985, to study contemporary social, political and economic issues and problems in an inter-disciplinary perspective and to make available its findings and recommendations to government bodies, social scientists, policy makers, people's and workers' organisations, so as to widen their options for action. The evolution of an informed and action-oriented public opinion is the primary aim of the Institute.

The research projects undertaken by the Institute cover a wide range of subjects in the areas of local governance, women's studies, environment and contemporary economic and political issues. The Institute also organises seminars, workshops, discussions and training programmes for the exchange of ideas and dissemination of its research findings.

The major research thrust of the Institute is in the areas of Local Governance (Panchayati Raj), Urban Studies, Women's Studies, Economic Affairs, Human Rights and Police Reforms and International Studies. We seek to build a community of concerned scholars and activists engaged in ushering in a humane and just society.

About the Editor

Dr. George Mathew is the Founder Director of the Institute of Social Sciences, New Delhi. He is specializing on the local government system, decentralization and gender equity.

Two Decades of New Panchayati Raj in Karnataka

Issues, Options and Lessons

Edited by
George Mathew

Published for

Institute of Social Sciences

by

CONCEPT PUBLISHING COMPANY PVT. LTD., NEW DELHI-110059

This project was made possible by grants from
Government of Karnataka and World Bank (SIDA Trust Fund)

ISBN-13: 978-81-8069-768-5 (PB)

First Published 2011

Published and Printed by

Since 1974

Concept Publishing Company Pvt. Ltd.
Regd. Office:
A/15-16, Commercial Block, Mohan Garden,
New Delhi-110059 (INDIA)
Phones: 25351460, 25351794, *Fax*: 091-11-25357109
Email: publishing@conceptpub.com,
Website: www.conceptpub.com

Editorial Office:
H-13, Bali Nagar, New Delhi-110 015, India.

Cataloging in Publication Data--*Courtesy*: D.K. Agencies (P) Ltd. <docinfo@dkagencies.com>

Two decades of new panchayati raj in Karnataka : issues, options and lessons / edited by George Mathew.
p. cm.
Includes index.
ISBN 9788180697678

1. Panchayat--India--Karnataka--History--Congresses. 2. Rural development--India- -Karnataka--Congresses. I. Mathew, George, 1943- II. Institute of Social Sciences (New Delhi, India)

DDC 320.8095487 22

Dedicated in the memory of
L.C. Jain
one of the pioneers of the
Panchayati Raj system

Contents

SECTION VI
Concluding Session

Introduction

Though Karnataka has a long history of rural self-governance, it is the Karnataka Zilla Parishads, Taluk Panchayat Samithis, Mandal Panchayats and Nyaya Panchayats Act, 1983 enacted by the Janata Government under the leadership of Ramakrishna Hegde and Abdul Nazir Sab that revolutionized the concept of democratic decentralisation below the State level. Abdul Nazir Sab was not very wrong when he said, that it was this promise of '*Power to the People*' that was mainly responsible for the Janata Party's return to power in the elections held to the State legislative assembly in 1985. That the people of Karnataka overwhelmingly welcomed the move was evident when between 60-75 per cent of the voters turned out to elect their representatives to these institutions.

The constitution of 19 Zilla Parishads and 2,535 Mandal Panchayats and the election of 887 Zilla Parishad members and 54,688 Mandal Panchayat members, and their empowerment in 1987 ushered in decentralisation of governance on a scale not seen earlier in the State, or probably in the country. In a way, it inspired the then Prime Minister Rajiv Gandhi and later Prime Ministers V.P. Singh and P.V. Narasimha Rao to attempt to accord a constitutional status to the Panchayati Raj institutions by amending the Constitution.

A national seminar was held in Delhi on 26th and 27th October, 1985. The theme was "Decentralisation of Power—The Karnataka Model". Eminent protagonists of democratic decentralisation like S.K. Dey and prominent intellectuals like Malcom Adisheshaiah, D.T. Lakdawala, Nirmal K. Mukherji, Upendra Baxi and Abdul Nazir Sab, spoke in the seminar. Speaker after speaker in that seminar expressed their appreciation for the bold step that the Government of Karnataka had taken in enacting the 1985 Act and expressed their hope that the experiment will succeed and become a role model for democratic decentralisation for the entire country.

However, the euphoria was short lived. With the untimely death of Abdul Nazir Sab and the fall of the Ramakrishna Hegde Government, the downward slide of the Panchayats started in Karnataka. The Karnataka Panchayat Raj Act, 1993, enacted by the Karnataka legislative assembly to conform to the Constitution 73rd Amendment Act, was a mere shadow of the 1983 Act. Both the Janata and the Congress parties devised all kinds of stratagems to dilute, disempower, marginalize, destabilize and sabotage the Panchayats – bringing Panchayats under the administrators, not holding elections on time, reducing the term of the Presidents and the Vice Presidents, creating and strengthening parallel bodies – all these and much more happened in the decade that followed. Many a time public spirited citizens, a few elected representatives of the Panchayati Raj institutions and on at least two occasions, the State Election Commission itself had to approach the judiciary to compel the State Government to hold elections.

According to many researchers on governance, Karnataka which was once a pathbreaker in democratic decentralisation, became a role model for emasculating the Panchayats in spirit as well as in substance. There is reluctance on the part of the legislators to let power percolate to the sub-State levels. The legislators had amended the 1993 Act to empower the Gram Sabhas to select beneficiaries under the various schemes of the State Government. Fearing that the process would reduce their importance and powers, these very legislators later proposed another amendment to the Act to take away that power from the Gram Sabhas and vest it in committees headed by themselves.

In session after session of the assembly for years on end, the legislators in the guise of debating the performance of the State Government, criticised the Panchayats for not holding Gram Sabhas properly and not selecting the beneficiaries, resulting in the non-utilisation of the funds meant to reach the beneficiaries, particlularly of the *Ashraya* —a State Government sponsored housing scheme for rural areas. Instead of debating the ways and means of strengthening the Gram Sabhas and ensuring their timely holding, the legislators only thought of divesting them of that power and vesting it in themselves.

The Panchayati Raj in Karnataka slid from a pristine position to an apology for democratic decentralisation within a short span of twenty years. It is in this background of the continuous erosion of the powers of the Panchayats that a need was felt to take a look back and assess what was happening to the Panchayati Raj institutions and deliberate on what should be done to arrest the downward trend. The result of this thinking was the organisation of a convention of elected representatives of Panchayati Raj institutions, civil society leaders and wellwishers of the system in Karnataka to discuss these and many other issues confronting these institutions.

The support that the idea of such a convention received from the elected members of all the three tiers of the Panchayati Raj institutions, the leaders of the civil society, well meaning friends and the bureaucracy showed the concern every one had for the Panchayati Raj institutions. The convention, which was a sequel to the national seminar held in 1985 at Delhi, was held in the sprawling *Jnana Jyoti* Auditorium of the Bangalore University on 1st and 2nd of April, 2007; and was addressed by prominent intellectuals and ministers and officers of the Central and State governments. More than 1,000 elected members and office bearers of all the three tiers of the Panchayati Raj institutions, members of the civil society and sympathizers actively participated in the event. Many activists working with Panchayats in Karnataka were unanimous on strengthening the Panchayat system cutting across all political party ideologies because Gram Swaraj alone can be the best foundation for Karnataka's progress and prosperity. Quoting Mahatama Gandhi's famous quote "A policy is a temporary principle and principle is a permanent policy" many participants argued that as a matter of principle Panchayats have to be strengthened because they are the best instruments for bringing rural prosperity in Karnataka.

This book tries to capture the spirit of the churning that took place during the two days of the convention. We are extremely grateful to the Government of Karnataka for all the support extended for this conference. We acknowledge with gratitude the grant received from the World Bank (SIDA Trust Fund) for this project. Thanks are due to the staff of the Bangalore Office of the Institute of Social Sciences. Several young volunteers helped in meticulously transcribing the speeches, translating and editing them and preparing the manuscript for publication. Special thanks are due to Bapu Heddurshetti, V.K. Nataraj, Manu Kulkarni and Joya Roy for going through the manuscript and giving their valuable suggestions.

The Contributors

Mani Shankar Aiyar

Minister for Panchayati Raj, Sports and North Eastern Development, Government of India

C.M. Udasi

Minister for Rural Development and Panchayati Raj, Government of Karnataka

Leeladevi R. Prasad

Former Minister, Government of Karnataka

A.G. Kodagi

Chairman, State Finance Commission, Government of Karnataka

U.R. Ananthamurthy

Chairman, Institute of Social Sciences and Jnanapeetha Awardee

C. Narayanaswamy

Former Chairman, Bangalore Rural Zilla Parishad and Former Member, Lok Sabha

Savita Ramesh

Former Vice President, Chikmagalur Zilla Panchayat

Geeta Sethi

Programme Coordinator, Social Development Unit, The World Bank

M.P. Prakash

Minister for Home, Law, Human Rights and Parliamentary Affairs, Government of Karnataka

Abdul Rahim Rather

Leader of the Opposition, Jammu and Kashmir Legislative Assembly

M.R. Sreenivasa Murthy

Principal Secretary, Rural Development and Panchayati Raj, Government of Karnataka

S.S. Meenakshisundaram

Former Secretary to Government of India, Ministry of Rural Development

M.R. Hegde

Election Commissioner, Karnataka

Na. Li. Krishna

Chairman, Nagarakere Gram Panchayat, Maddur Taluk, Mandya District

K. Ravikumar

Chairman, Kyathaghatta Gram Panchayat, Maddur Taluk,

Mandya District

H.B. Madhusudhan

Secretary, Annur Gram Panchayat, Maddur Taluk, Mandya District

Kamala

Chairman, Jodihosahalli Gram Panchayat, Kunigal Taluk, Tumkur District

Krishna M. Ittangi

Vice Chairman, Bhagya Nagar Gram Panchayat, Koppal District

S.R. Hiremath

Samaj Parivartana Samudaya, Dharwar

S.A. Ravindranath

Minister for Rural Water Supply, Sanitation and Sugar, Government of Karnataka

George Mathew

Director, Institute of Social Sciences, New Delhi

SECTION I
Inaugural Session

1

The Need to Look Back

George Mathew

It is my honour and privilege to welcome you all to this conference on "Two Decades of New Panchayati Raj in Karnataka : Issues, Options and Lessons." My thoughts go back to the early 1980's. The dominant thinking at that time was how to give "power to the people". The great masses of people are in the villages of India and the best instrumentality to give power to the people was the Panchayats. The Asoka Mehta Committee and the West Bengal initiative in the second half of 70's had created a momentum for this idea.

In 1983, Karnataka showed the way under the leadership of the then Chief Minister Ramakrishna Hegde and the Panchayati Raj Minister, Abdul Nazir Sab, as to what a State can do to bring in radical changes to give power to the people. Ramakrishna Hegde and Abdul Nazir Sab, at that time, revolutionised the concept of district administration. The whole idea of district government creating a third stratum in Indian federalism came into vogue then. Today the Administrative Reforms Commission under the chairmanship of Veerappa Moily is very seriously looking into this whole question of district government. The leaders of Karnataka in the mid-80s took steps to bring about gender equality and for the first time in the country or, for that matter, anywhere in the world, 25 per cent of seats were reserved for women in local government bodies. This had extraordinary impact all over the country.

The Constitutional Amendment

In October 1985, while addressing the national seminar on 'Decentralization of Power—The Karnataka Model,' held by the Institute of Social Sciences at the India International Centre, New Delhi, Abdul Nazir Sab said: "Our intention to bring about a radical structural change in the governance of our State may be laudable, but without a constitutional amendment guaranteeing the "Four Pillar State", our efforts may not be as fruitful as we desire. In my opinion this is the major question the intellectuals of this country must ponder over".[1]

At the national level, two young leaders of that time realized the need to take the idea forward and worked ceaselessly to bring about what became the historic 73rd and 74th Constitution Amendment Acts. One of those, Mani Shankar Aiyar, is with us today. The other visionary was Rajiv Gandhi. His conviction, commitment, hard work and persistent efforts supported by Mani Shankar Aiyar finally resulted in the revolutionary constitutional amendments.

After this great leap forward by the State of Karnataka, giving power to the people, this State became a pilgrim centre for the Panchayati Raj advocates. They started visiting this State. Andhra Pradesh followed suit with the slogan "Taking the government and administration to the doorsteps of the people". The Jammu & Kashmir government sent a high-power delegation to Karnataka to study the model Panchayat system here, under the leadership of Mohammed Shafi, who was then Panchayati Raj Minister and today we have with us his successor, A.R. Rather, from Jammu & Kashmir. Jammu & Kashmir did a great thing by following the example of Karnataka.

The Need to Look Back

After the 1983 Act, almost a quarter of a century has passed. Fourteen years have passed since the 73rd Amendment became part of the Constitution of India. In Karnataka, the new Panchayats officially assumed power on April 1, 1987. Twenty years have passed since then. And some of us, looking at this situation, realized the significance of this time and we thought that the twenty years' journey of Karnataka's Panchayati Raj should be looked into and the opportunities and possibilities of the last twenty years in Karnataka explored.

I shared this idea with Mani Shankar Aiyar in New Delhi and he was very enthusiastic about this programme. In Bangalore I had meetings with senior officials in the government and the friends of Karnataka Panchayati Raj. The support was overwhelming. I must especially mention C.M. Udasi, Minister for Rural Development and Panchayati Raj, Government of Karnataka; M.R. Sreenivasa Murthy, Principal Secretary, Rural Development and Panchayati Raj, Government of Karnataka; C. Narayanaswamy, S.S. Meenakshisundaram, V.K. Nataraj, B.S. Bhargava and many others who came forward to support this idea.

The World Bank has a pioneering project on strengthening Panchayats in Karnataka. When I broached the idea of such a programme to Geetha Sethi, who is here with us today—she is especially in charge of the project—the Bank was very positive about the programme. Although keeping a low profile, the Bank has been a big supporter of decentralization in India.

I must sincerely acknowledge the fact that this programme today was made possible by the hard work, commitment and dedication of a large number of friends and well wishers in the Union and State Governments, voluntary organisations and research institutes.

We have a very distinguished guest today for our inaugural function. U.R. Ananthamurthy, an eminent son of Karnataka, a close associate of Abdul Nazir Sab and an advocate of all progressive ideas, is presiding over this function. We are honoured by the presence of Mani Shankar Aiyar, the Union Minister for Panchayati Raj. I sometimes wonder how he is managing three very important ministries in the country, Panchayati Raj, Sports and North-Eastern Development. But his first love is Panchayati Raj. The innovative programmes that he has introduced all over the country since he assumed charge of the Ministry of Panchayati Raj, in the last more than two and a half years, have attracted the attention of not only the whole country but of the whole world.

We are very happy that C.M. Udasi, is with us for this function. When I wrote a letter to him immediately after we decided to hold this function, he called me over phone and expressed his full support for this effort. He also said that when Abdul Nazir Sab and others were introducing and taking this idea forward, he was an MLA and Udasi is an MLA in this Assembly for the last 25 years or so and I am told that he is a man of the people, a man who understands the ground realities.

A.G. Kodagi is another popular leader of Karnataka. He is a former MLA. Most of you know that he got elected as member of Zilla Parishad in 1987 and served as the Chairman of the Standing Committee on Education. He is a man who is dedicated to the cause of Panchayati Raj and Rural Development. Presently he is heading the State Finance Commission.

Smt. Leeladevi Prasad, former Minister and senior leader in the State working for the cause of women and their empowerment, is championing the cause of women's reservation in the legislative assemblies and the Parliament. She is active in various social, cultural and women's organizations.

We have two distinguished members of the Administrative Service here, our senior officials as guests of honour, Falguni Rajkumar, Additional Chief Secretary and Development Commissioner, Government of Karnataka and M.R. Srineevasa Murthy, Secretary, Panchayati Raj, Government of Karnataka. Their support for this programme was very special and whenever I approached them for their help in making this programme a great success they were there and spared no efforts and I am extremely grateful to these senior officials of the Karnataka Government for helping us with this programme.

I specially welcome all the Panchayat Presidents, Vice Presidents and Members, who have come from all the districts of the State and the members of civil society organizations and concerned citizens who are here. With this level of participation, I am very sure that we will have a very fruitful debate and discussion in the coming two days.

NOTE

1. Abdul Nazir Sab, 'Towards a Four-Pillar State', in *Panchayati Raj in Karnataka Today : Its National Dimensions* . George Mathew (Ed.), Institute of Social Sciences and Concept Publishing Company, New Delhi, 1986.

2

Two Steps Forward, One Step Backward

Mani Shankar Aiyar

The history of Panchayati Raj in India has been signposted by three very eminent persons : Mahatma Gandhi, Jawaharlal Nehru and Rajiv Gandhi. But the architects of Panchayati Raj below this policy direction are also a handful of very distinguished persons. First, Balwantrai Mehta; second, S.K. Dey; third, Asoka Mehta; and undoubtedly, the fourth must be Abdul Nazir Sab. I give Abdul Nazir Sab this high position of significance in Panchayati Raj because in implementing the Panchayati Raj system he was genuinely a pioneer, someone who blazed a completely new trail. It is a terrible tragedy that he was the Panchayati Raj minister in Karnataka for only a very short time, but even in the few years that he was able to exercise his powers in the ministry, he set Karnataka on a completely different course to the rest of the country, and it is the rest of the country that is now following that course.

The government to which Abdul Nazir Sab belonged had come to power after inflicting a crushing defeat on the Congress Party in 1983. And that electoral success had been repeated at the beginning of 1985 after Rajiv Gandhi became the Prime Minister of India. The Chief Minister of Karnataka at that time was Ramakrishna Hegde with Rajiv Gandhi as the Prime Minister in Delhi. And yet it is a tribute to our democracy that the young new Prime Minister of India had an extremely close personal rapport with Chief Minister Ramakrishna Hegde notwithstanding the political differences between them. That personal rapport between the two of them played a major role in fulfilling the dream of Abdul Nazir Sab, as expressed in the quotation which we heard from Dr. George Mathew, of ensuring that Panchayati Raj did not remain merely a piece of State legislation but became an integral part of the Constitution.

Rajiv Gandhi and Responsive Administration

The innovativeness of what was being done in Karnataka caught the imagination of Prime Minister Rajiv Gandhi because, to his mind, the single most important domestic requirement of India, forty years after independence, was to secure an administration that was responsive to the people. The importance which Rajiv Gandhi gave to responsive administration is illustrated by the fact that in the first telecast address that he delivered to the nation as Prime Minister after the election of December 1984, he mentioned the issue of responsive administration at least half a dozen times in a very, very brief address of about half a dozen minutes. And, subsequently, when he recast his mother's 20-Point Programme, the 20th point in the 1986 20-Point Programme was "Responsive Administration."

But it was all very well to talk of responsive administration; the challenge was how does one establish a responsive administration? To find an answer to this question, Rajiv Gandhi convened five successive meetings of all the district magistrates of India in five different parts of the country. And it became very clear very early on that the brightest of the district magistrates said that the only way to get a responsive administration is to bring in Panchayati Raj as a constitutional obligation and the dimmer the IAS officer the less he wanted Panchayati Raj. After having listened to three sets of district magistrates, at the fourth meeting in Jaipur, Rajiv Gandhi summed up the lessons that he had learnt in the following words : "A responsive administration has to be a responsible administration and a responsible administration has to be a representative administration".

Rajiv Gandhi had reached this conclusion exactly one year after the Panchayati Raj system had been radicalised under Abdul Nazir Sab in Karnataka. And that is why after he had come to this conclusion in April 1988, he spent the next one and a half years thinking about how to extend the Karnataka experiment to the requirements of the country as a whole. Of course, the experience of other States of India was also taken into account, most notably that of West Bengal where there had been a consistent form of Panchayati Raj from about 1977 onwards, as also from States like Gujarat and Maharashtra where there had not been too much disruption of the earlier Panchayati Raj system.

Amending the Constitution

But the essence was that whatever lessons were learnt from other States these were adapted to the Karnataka system. It was the Karnataka system that was at the heart of how we would have Panchayati Raj through the Constitution in the country as a whole. And thus it came about that when on the 15th of May, 1989, Rajiv Gandhi presented the Constitution 64th Amendment Bill in the Lok Sabha, he specifically said that this draft bill was the consequence of a *manthan*—a churning—of all the experiences of all the States, the good experience and the bad experience, and by churning this nation-wide experience, he was producing this *amrit* called the 64th Amendment Bill.

And that is why although I returned only yesterday afternoon from a very long journey abroad, I overcame the objections of my family and said I must once again travel down to Bangalore in order to be present on this very important occasion, which I regard as one of the most important sources of constitutional Panchayati Raj in India : the 20th anniversary of the launching of Abdul Nazir Sab's new Panchayati Raj in Karnataka.

While those who are today in charge of the government in Karnataka, as well as those who belong to the political persuasion of Abdul Nazir Sab and all of you, thousands and thousands of people who have been elected to the Panchayati Raj institutions in Karnataka, deserve the praise and felicitations which I have come to bestow upon you, at the same time, since Karnataka was the pioneer of Panchayati Raj, there are some very special responsibilities that I would request you to acknowledge on the occasion of this 20th anniversary.

The first of these is that since it was Karnataka Panchayati Raj that rose first and the country followed, if Panchayati Raj in Karnataka slips then there is the danger of Panchayati Raj all over the country slipping. Unfortunately, it has been our experience over the last twenty years that every time the government in Karnataka changes, and it does not matter whether it changes from Udasi to me or from me to Udasi, every time a government in Karnataka changes, Panchayati Raj in Karnataka comes under threat. So, instead of moving forward smoothly, the movement of Panchayati Raj in Karnataka is always two steps forward, one step backward, then two steps forward and one step backward. Smooth progression to the top is not taking place in the State and that is why I am sorry to say, on this 20th anniversary, that there are other States in India which have overtaken Karnataka in Panchayati Raj.

This happens mostly because members of the Legislative Assemblies feel threatened by the Panchayati Raj representatives. I would have thought that after twenty years of Panchayati Raj, the MLAs of Karnataka, and, indeed, MLAs all over the country would have recognised that there is no threat to them from Panchayati Raj. As my leader, Smt. Sonia Gandhi, has said on the floor of Parliament, what this country needs is a strong central government, strong State governments and strong local governments. It is only if all the three tiers are strong that the country will be strong and we can move fast ahead. I would request the MLAs of Karnataka, and indeed MLAs from all over the country, to recognize that the chief difference between their jobs and that of the elected Panchayati Raj representatives is that MLAs are elected to legislate whereas Panchayati Raj representatives are elected to execute. That is the key difference; and if an MLA prefers to execute and does not find legislation interesting, then instead of standing for election to the Vidhan Soudha he should stand for election to the Zilla Panchayat.

Need to Demarcate the Powers

But I also blame very strongly the Government of Karnataka (and State governments all over India) for not making it clear as to what are the powers that belong to the Panchayati institutions and what are the powers that remain with the State government. The confusion results in MLAs feeling constantly threatened that their powers are being taken away. It should be decided once for all that these are the powers of the Panchayats; these are the powers of the State; and the remaining powers are the powers of the Centre. If only this is made completely clear, as it has long been made clear in the developed democracies, there would be no ground for any conflict between the Panchayat representatives and the MLAs.

Karnataka, in fact, under M.Y. Ghorpade, had produced the Panchayati Raj Act of 1993. In that Act all the 29 subjects mentioned in the Constitution were incorporated and, in fact, some other subjects were added and it was believed that the devolution was complete. But you know IAS officers don't take legislation seriously unless that legislation is transformed into a government order; and transforming the legislative provisions into government orders has been a very slow, a very halting business in the last twenty years. And frequently what is given with the left hand is taken away by the right hand because even more than the MLA it is the IAS officer who feels threatened. Now, since these IAS officers are very highly educated people and they still get very frightened of all the illiterate Panchayati Raj people, I don't agree with Mrs. Leeladevi that you should have educational qualifications!

I plead with you to move forward smoothly, harmoniously and without fear. Let me give you an example: Roads and National Highways: who can build them and maintain them except the Central Government? State highways: who can build them and maintain them except the State government? But major district roads: why can't the Zilla Panchayats do that? Other District Roads, why can't the Taluk Panchayats do that? And village roads: why can't the Gram Panchayats do that? That is all it takes. You take one subject. You see which activity should be done by the Centre, which activity should be done by the State, which activity should be done by the Zilla Panchayat, which activity by the Taluk Panchayat and which activity by the Gram Panchayat, and then freeze it, that this will not be changed.

This is how we are going to move forward. Then the MLA will know that the contract for the village road is only Rs. one lakh; the contract for the taluk road is only Rs. 5 lakh; and the contract for the district road is only Rs. one crore. But the contract for the State highway is Rs. 100 crore; then why bother about the village road? If in all 29 subjects, this kind of Activity Mapping is clearly done, then there would be no ground for conflict between groups. All of us need each other, all of us have to be friends with each other, and all of us will be moving forward together. That is what should be the focus of attention.

The second issue is that you must not allow any slippage. If devolution has taken place by one government, then it should not be taken back by another government. You can give more but, having given it, I think it should remain where it is. Otherwise there will always be uncertainty as to whether Panchayati Raj is going to progress or whether Panchayati Raj would suffer regression (*Applause*).

The March of Women in Panchayats

The next issue I wish to take up will not receive much applause. I want to draw your attention to the remarkable performance of women in the Karnataka's Panchayati Raj elections. According to the information given to me, although the reservation in Karnataka amounts to 33 per cent, the actual presence of women in the Panchayati Raj institutions is well over 40 per cent and at the lowest village level it varies between 44 and 47 per cent in different parts of Karnataka.

But even more remarkable than this overall performance is that at the village level, among the Scheduled Tribes, the percentage of women who have got elected, I am told, is about 65, double the quota meant for them. And then, among the Scheduled Castes, the percentage of women, I am told, in your village panchayats is a little over 50, although the quota is only 33 per cent. Finally, the Muslim women of Karnataka have definitely proved that the *hijab* does not stand in the way of standing for or winning an election, or running the administration. They have proved that Muslim women are equal to women from all other communities in running Panchayati Raj.

So, given this outstanding performance of women in Karnataka's Panchayati Raj, I have two suggestions to place before Minister Udasi regarding women in Panchayati Raj. First, in Bihar, reservation for women has been raised to 50 per cent. Madhya Pradesh has announced that they too are going to raise the percentage of reservation to 50. God Almighty has decided that half of us will be men and half of us will be women. If God had said, one-third girls and two-third boys, then the Constitution would have been enough. But since God has said half boys and half girls and Bihar, regarded as a backward State, and Madhya Pradesh, not often regarded as an advanced State, have moved so far ahead, does Karnataka have the courage to raise the percentage of reservation for women from 33 to 50? And if Minister Udasi is not willing to accept my suggestion, let me warn him that the women of Karnataka are doing so well in Panchayati Raj that the next demand is going to come from men that there should be reservation for men!

The second request I want to place before Minister Udasi with regard to women in Panchayati Raj is that now the system is of changing the reservation every 5 years, which means that a girl who gets experience in Panchayati Raj is then forced to stand in a general seat or just leave the Panchayati Raj system and all her experience and education just goes completely waste. Now Mr. Udasi, you have been a member for your assembly constituency for how many years – 25 years? And nobody dropped you by saying now the girls will come in. So, what we need is a fair and just system. The experience of Tamil Nadu, if you will accept the experience of Tamil Nadu, has been to reserve a seat for women for at least 10 years. I think it should be made 15 years. Then the women who get elected will learn by experience and then they can use that experience much more effectively for the good of Panchayati Raj.

Tasks Ahead

There is one more suggestion, which is of a general nature. You are now splitting the 5 years for which a person is elected as the president into two or three different periods. I think the president should be given a full five year term.

I was hoping to inaugurate during my present visit the last computer in the villages. If full connectivity is achieved, we should be able to give more grants. I have praised the Mysore experiment in satellite communication all over the country and the world. I have recently inaugurated a similar studio in West Bengal. In the New Zealand conference of local bodies, I have praised your Mysore experiment.

My final request is that Karnataka, which has over the last twenty years built up a cadre of excellent officers in Panchayati Raj, should somehow ensure that what these officers know about Panchayati Raj reaches as a message to the rest of the country. So I would request you to be liberal in making available experienced Panchayati Raj officers from Karnataka for other States which have not learnt how to run Panchayati Raj as effectively as you have.

And, in conclusion, may I extent to all of you gathered here my heartiest congratulations on this very auspicious occasion and request you to please remember that the extent to which you do your jobs honestly and with dedication to your people, to that extent you will win your next election!

3

Our Expectations and Your Responsibilities

C.M. Udasi

When the Panchayati Raj system was initiated in 1983 I had been elected a member of the legislative assembly. Abdul Nazir Sab had great concern for the Panchayati Raj system, he had great expectations from it. He invited S.K. Dey to a meeting of the members of the legislative assembly and discussed about the Panchayati Raj system in detail. Since he felt that the decisions taken in the Gram Sabhas would be the best decisions, he hoped that there will be revolutionary changes in the State. I had expressed one of my doubts even at that time. I had wondered how far it was practical to conduct Gram Sabhas in villages with a population of more than 500. You are more experienced than me. If we have to strengthen the Gram Sabhas and get them to prepare the plans for the villages to be implemented by the Gram Panchayats, if the money received from the State government is to be properly utilized, you know to what heights we have to reach. If this becomes successful then it will be possible to bring about a new and an overall change in the Panchayati Raj system.

You have been elected as Panchayat members and have been involved for the last one and a half years in the administration. After Section 90 of the Karnataka Panchayati Raj Act came into force, we have conducted three elections to all the three tiers of the system. You also must have noticed that we have brought so many amendments to the Act. Though we have been suggesting to you that the resources should be mobilized depending on the requirements and that they should be properly utilized, the implementation of this depends on your commitment. With a view to see that the training being given through satellite by the Rural Development Centre in Mysore started by Abdul Nazir Sab is successful in all the taluks, the Government has decided to start the training programme in five places in Karnataka in the next few days.

Your Responsibilities

When a grant of Rs. 2 lakh is received by the Gram Panchayat, instead of deciding on the priorities and implementing them, the members are busy distributing the money among themselves saying that they will get the necessary things done in their wards with that money. You will have to seriously consider whether development is possible if this happens. The reality in these meetings is different from what is on paper. This should not happen. While in the beginning the grants released to the Panchayati Raj institutions were of the order of Rs. 3,689 crore, the amount disbursed has now reached Rs. 4,900 crore. Since the Panchayati Raj institutions have to spend so much money in one financial year, it is your responsibility to see that the money is spent properly. This is your tax payers' money. This is not your money. You have the responsibility to see that the money is not spent wrongly.

In the background of these experiences, you have to suggest as to what changes have to be brought about. Programmes have to be simplified. The development works in the State have to be transferred to the Panchayati Raj institutions as early as possible. For this reason, these institutions are being given more funds. In the year 2004-2005 we have released a sum of Rs. 1,596 crore for the implementation of various schemes. This amount has become Rs. 4,360 crore in the year 2006. We are planning to release Rs. 4,951 crore in the year 2007-2008. But the money will have to be utilized properly. We have to enhance the capabilities of the Panchayats so that the money is properly used.

Kodagi has said that the Panchayats have been given the powers, they have been given the funds, but the government has failed or is delaying to provide the necessary staff. It is a fact that there is a dearth of experienced officers. There are examples of the water man or the tax collector being made the Secretary of the Gram Panchayat in many places. You have been complaining that these secretaries are unable to work properly; they are unable to implement the programmes successfully.

Education for Panchayat Members

Leeladevi Prasad said that we should prescribe a minimum educational qualification of SSLC for the members of the panchayats. You must have wondered as to why there should be a minimum educational qualification for the members of the Panchayats when no such qualification is prescribed for the members of the legislative assemblies and the Parliament. The only qualification required of a person contesting elections to the legislative assembly is that he should be 25 years old and should not be insane. However, at the end Leeladevi said that at least 7th or 8th Standard should be prescribed as minimum qualification. She might have said that to cover me as I have studied only up to 8th Standard!

In this context I would like to tell you one thing. Though education is important, more important is the commitment. There should be commitment, to the position I have been elected to, to those who have elected me, whose problems I should seek to solve with every opportunity available to me. Within the funds received and the available income, what can I do, what is my aim? These are some of the questions which you should ask yourselves. Along with education we require common sense. It is said that most of the criminals are educated people. Please do not think that I am speaking like this because I have passed only the 8th

Standard. But at the same time we cannot say that education is not necessary. If we do not know how to read and write, it is possible that the Secretaries may mislead us, other officers may mislead us. We have to agree that education is absolutely necessary.

We will give Women their Due

I also wish to respond to the issues raised by the Union Minister for Panchayati Raj. I completely agree with him that there should be 50 per cent reservation for women. We will discuss this issue in the cabinet and implement it. When I had been to Orissa, I saw that there they have a system in which if the President of a Panchayat is a man, then the Vice President is a woman, and if the President is a woman, then the Vice President is a man. This is compulsory there. This is also just. I will try to implement it in Karnataka also. We will discuss this issue in the cabinet and implement it.

Duration of Offices

The Union Minister has said that the term of office of the Presidents and Vice Presidents should be a full 5 years instead of 20 months or 30 months. I wish to bring to your notice what happens if this is done. I hope it has already come to the notice of the Union Minister. We decided to have a 20 months term because of our concern for social justice, so that persons belonging to different categories get an opportunity. But in many places the offices have been divided into 8 months and 12 months. What is to be done if the same thing happens when the term of office is made 5 years? What is to be done if within 5 years there are 5 Presidents and 5 Vice Presidents? If the elders in your village or the leaders of your party insist that 5 persons should be made Presidents in 5 years what can you do? So if we only fix the term at 5 years it will be of no use. The term can be fixed at 5 years only if the President is elected directly. You have to seriously consider this. On an experimental basis I want to introduce direct elections for the presidentship of Gram Panchayats and see how it works.

The Union Minister has said that he had a desire to connect the last computer in the villages of Karnataka. We have not been able to fulfil his desire. You also may be aware about what has happened in the case of computers. It is necessary that every village should have a computer and should be directly connected. I also have a desire to connect all 5,600 Gram Panchayats with computers and take the Union Minister to my village to inaugurate the last computer.

He has also said that we should spare the services of some officers for use in other States. We still have to bring so many reforms in the system in our State. We have to curb corruption. We have to make the administration transparent. For this we require the services of experienced officers. At this juncture if we send our experienced officers outside the State, then again we will have to spend a lot of time in gaining experience. After we bring about all these reforms in our State we may become a model State in Panchayati Raj system. I request the Union Minister to bear with us till then.

Today and tomorrow, on these two days, we have to find solutions to many problems during the discussions. We have to see that in the coming days the plans are successfully formulated and that they reach the people. I wish to promise you that the Government will consider your suggestions with all the respect they deserve. Thank you !

4

The Rural Dream of 'Neer Sab'

Leeladevi R. Prasad

My *Suvarna Karnataka* greetings to all. The Panchayati Raj system has become a twenty years old huge tree today. It can also be seen as a twenty years old young maiden. Before I speak about the people who have shaped this system in the last twenty years, I wish to say a few words in memory of Ramakrishna Hegde and Abdul Nazir Sab. Ramakrishna Hegde became the Chief Minister in 1983. I still remember that Abdul Nazir Sab was not even an MLC then. The Chief Minister called him to the Kumara Kripa guest house and said that he wanted to make Nazir Sab a minister first and then an MLC, that he wanted Nazir Sab to take the Rural Development and Panchayati Raj ministry.

How Nazir Sab became Neer Sab

Udasi and I were then only MLAs and not ministers. I wish to share with you two of my experiences while we were working with Ramakrishna Hegde and Abdul Nazir Sab. My constituency was a dry constituency. There was no water. About six months after Abdul Nazir Sab became minister, I told him that the women in our villages walk miles together to fetch water, that they are facing a lot of hardship, that he should visit my constituency once. Then I took him to my constituency. He was such a great man, he came to my constituency. Whenever an important person comes to a village, the tradition is to welcome him by pouring water on his feet. This is our culture. When he came, the women in our villages came with pots full of water and started pouring on his feet. The day was very hot. Women had brought water from far-off places. Nazir Sab stopped those women and said, *"My mothers! Why are you wasting water by pouring it on my feet ? You say that there is no water in your villages. I have come to give you water not to get it wasted on my feet"*.

I am also a very obstinate woman. After this promise by him, I got 1,200 bore wells dug in my constituency with his help.

I can never forget Nazir Sab. When he came back from Bombay, he stayed in the Kumara Kripa guest house. I went to enquire about his health. He was lying on his deathbed. I told him that God will make him well. He said, *Leelamma, I had visited that village in your constituency. Did you get water for that village?* I became so emotional then. What a fine mind he had. He was about to die in a day or two and he was enquiring about water in my village. How can I forget such a great man? That is why he is known as ***Neer Sab***. (*Neer* is water in Kannada.)

Even now so many villages in Karnataka are suffering from lack of water and womenfolk know it better than men. Even today many women walk miles together to fetch water. Wherever Nazir Sab got bore wells dug, we do get water there. But sometimes there is no water, or even if water is there, there is no electricity. All of us are experiencing this every day. During this rainy season you should do rainwater harvesting in the memory of Abdul Nazir Sab. You should see that every bore well is recharged with rain water.

The Initial Hurdles for Women

If Ramakrishna Hegde and Abdul Nazir Sab had not made the women experience the benefits of democratic decentralization, and not brought in the new Panchayati Raj system, women in Karnataka could not have made much progress. If women are getting so many opportunities today, the Panchayati Raj system is responsible for it.

Politically the power should not be there in the Centre. It should also not be in Bangalore. It should not be at the district level also. It should reach the last person in the last village. The credit for promoting this concept of decentralization of power should go to Karnataka. Karnataka today is in the forefront. We should not forget that following our example the Constitution 73rd Amendment was drafted. Rajiv Gandhi took the Karnataka model as an example and brought about amendments to the Constitution. But unfortunately it has stopped there. It is unfortunate that women have not yet been given reservations in the State assemblies and the Parliament.

On 1st April, 1987, the Panchayati Raj institutions in Karnataka assumed power. Immediately we organized training camps for those who got elected to the Panchayati Raj institutions. Many people had a problem. They said, *"Madam, you have brought the women from out of their homes. You made them climb the stage in the Panchayats. After all that what can they do?* I told them, *more than forty years have passed since independence. For 40 years you only have ruled. Let women also get some power now.* Then they ridiculed me by saying, *"Madam, where will you get so many women candidates?* I said *why can we not get them? You menfolk stay at home. Let your sister contest, let your wife contest, let your mother contest"*.

Saying thus we brought out women who were sitting at home and made them contest elections. We made them win. As a result of this today so many women have grown into mature politicians. Women who had not seen the road outside, women who had not seen the sunlight, women who had never visited a Panchayat office, a taluk office, are today going to all these places. In every village, in every taluk office, women can be seen running around with files tucked under their arms. This sight fills me with joy. What better results do you want?

Education for Panchayat Members

But still there are shortcomings. Many women do not have

education. Not that all men who get elected to the Panchayati Raj institutions are educated. Though 20 years have elapsed after the Panchayati Raj system came to our villages there are elected male members who still use their thumb impressions. I wish that by the time we celebrate the silver jubilee of Panchayati Raj in Karnataka there should be no member who is not educated. This is my desire. I wish to make a personal suggestion to Mani Shankar Aiyar. I request that at least SSLC should be made the minimum educational qualification for those contesting the Panchayati Raj elections. If they do not have education, they will have to put their thumb impression wherever the officers or the secretaries say.

This situation should not arise, at least in the future. I request that necessary amendments to the law should be brought to implement this. Let the candidates be at least 7th or 8th Standard pass. Education is necessary for all. It is necessary for legislators also and for parliamentarians also. We will say the same thing to them: if you do not have education, how will you know what is a budget, what is an agenda, what is written in those papers? My desire is that before going to the meetings, the members should first read these papers, understand them and then only go to the meetings. My desire is that in my country all should be educated, all should be literate. If we have to lead a normal life, it is necessary that we should be literate.

Panchayats shall grow

This system has to grow to new heights in Karnataka. The people of Karnataka have to shoulder this responsibility. They should join hands to improve their villages, their constituencies, and their environment. The rural scene must change. We see shortages of toilets in many villages. The Government is giving limitless funds for construction of toilets. If the primary necessities like the toilets, roads, schools, water, etc., are available in our villages, our villages will become ideal villages. People sitting in Vidhana Soudha do not have the power to do this. This power rests with the people working in the Gram Panchayats. You should hold on to the rudder of power in your villages, and change the villages radically and turn them into ideal villages. I had written two books about four years ago as to how the Panchayati Raj system grew right in front of our eyes. I had given a lot of statistics in them to prove my points. I wish to conclude by assuring George Mathew that when he organizes the silver jubilee celebrations of the Panchayati Raj in Karnataka he will surely notice fundamental changes in our Panchayati Raj system and in our villages.

5

Towards Fiscal Autonomy

A.G. Kodagi

Before we speak about the Panchayati Raj system in Karnataka it is necessary that we understand what the Panchayati Raj system or decentralization in India was like earlier. Before independence, decentralized method was used to ensure that the administration of the country was carried out smoothly.

During the British rule, administration was carried on through the District Boards and Taluk Boards. The District Boards in existence at that time carried on the administration of the entire district as district governments. In the same way, the Taluk Boards were entrusted with the responsibility of the entire Taluk and they were given supreme powers.

After independence, centralized plans were brought into being. But then, the basic problems of poverty alleviation, drinking water, population explosion, shortage of food-grains, etc., became more severe. In 1957, the Balwantrai Mehta Committee was appointed to find solutions to these problems. The committee recommended that an appropriate system of decentralized administration should be adopted and the administration should be handed over to elected local autonomous bodies. Later on, emphasizing the same point, the Asoka Mehta Committee laid the foundations for the unique Panchayati Raj system in the country.

In the year 1959, The Mysore Village Panchayats and Local Boards Act came into force. The Taluk Board was very powerful and had full financial autonomy. Unfortunately, slowly, both financial and administrative powers were taken away by the State government and financial autonomy became a mockery. There was also no elected body at the district level and hence the decentralization was not complete.

The Mandate of the Constitution

While framing the Indian Constitution our forefathers and political leaders gave importance to local self-government by special mention in Article 40 which reads: "The State shall take steps to organize village panchayats and endow them with such powers and authority that may be necessary to enable them to function as units of self-government."

When we examine Article 40, it becomes clear that the framers of our Constitution gave importance to the Panchayati Raj system. But it is also clear that the ruling government did not give any importance to the purpose of the framers of the Constitution or even to the Rama Rajya of Gandhiji's dreams. Though local government system was in place in many States, there was no uniform law and it is unfortunate that proper interest was not shown in giving them effective economic autonomy.

But in Karnataka, under the leadership of the late Abdul Nazir Sab, an effective Panchayati Raj system came into being. In 1985, Zilla Parishads, Taluk Panchayat Samitis, Mandal Panchayats and Nyaya Panchayats Act came into force. The Zilla Parishad had more economic autonomy and it could administratively play an effective role in the district. This law was responsible for implementing the principle of decentralization of power. But then, as time passed, the government tried to take away the powers of the Zilla Parishads one by one and this administered a death blow to the principle of decentralization.

In order to avoid the onslaught on the Panchayati Raj system in the country, after a long debate, two important amendments were brought to the Constitution in 1992 in the Parliament. Through the 73rd and 74th Amendments to the Constitution, efforts were made to provide a sound foundation to the principle of decentralization and the system of local self-government for the first time in the history of this country. Important changes complementing the Panchayati Raj system were brought in and the functions and responsibilities to be entrusted to the Panchayati Raj institutions were detailed in the schedules.

Three points were particularly added in these amendments :

1. Election Commissions were sought to be created for holding elections to the local bodies from time to time;
2. Provision was made for determining the share of these bodies in the resources of the State and for disbursing the same; and
3. A uniform law was sought to be brought in all over the country.

The Karnataka Act

In this background, in 1993, Karnataka also enacted a Panchayati Raj Act. The aim of this law was to create a three-tier Panchayati Raj system to elicit a higher level of participation by the people, ensure the effective implementation of the rural development programmes, and enable them to function as units of local self-government.

In this Act, as amended later, the Ward Sabhas in the Panchayat area were given more importance. Opportunity was provided in the Ward Sabhas to decide on all the basic requirements of life in the rural areas. They were given the responsibility of preparing local plans, selecting the beneficiaries and preparing programmes in response to the problems of people living below the poverty line. The Zilla Panchayats and Taluk Panchayats were empowered to implement the State and Central schemes. In the same way, Zilla Panchayats were also given the powers for preparing the district plans and implementing them. But the power to mobilize resources was given only to Gram Panchayats. Resources were sought to be provided to the local bodies from the State and the Centre. In totality, the local bodies were shaped in a way to conform to the principle of decentralization of power.

There is some truth in what is expressed by eminent leaders that at different levels, local self-governments are not in a position to take up responsibility and do justice to the people. In this context, the Ministry of Panchayati Raj commissioned the NCAER, the National Council for Applied Economic Research, to develop a working devolution index for Panchayati Raj institutions at the State level. Functions, finances and functionaries are the three dimensions equally important in achieving effective decentralization.

At this time, the government began its efforts to curb the powers of the panchayats. The rivalry for power began among the representatives of the panchayats. The hunger to monopolize power became evident. The government started issuing circulars. The illegal circulars and the interference by the officers increased. The Chief Executive Officers of the Zilla Panchayats were sent circulars directly and orders were issued to them directly ignoring the Zilla Panchayats. The result of all this was the clear proof of neglect of the Panchayati Raj institutions and the local bodies.

The Defects and the Solutions

The reasons for continuing defects in the Panchayati Raj system are several. They include :

1. Lack of awareness among the representatives of the people;
2. Lack of interest in development works;
3. Lack of resources;

4. Lack of staff;
5. Behaviour (misbehaviour) of officers;
6. Party politics;
7. Scope for corruption;
8. Lukewarm response to Ward Sabhas;
9. Lack of support by legislators; and
10. Unnecessary interference by the government.

Solutions to each of the above problems can be listed :

1. Proper guidance, training classes and proper knowledge of the law to the people's representatives;
2. Encouragement to take interest in the development process, proper information and participation in development;
3. Opportunity for mobilizing resources, their proper utilization and guidance;
4. Appointment of experienced staff and providing the opportunity to appoint them;
5. Proper guidance to the officers, proper instructions and making them aware of the fact that they are the servants of the people and instructing them not to interfere unnecessarily;
6. Trying to inculcate the feeling that after the elections there is no relationship between the parties and the development process and informing the representatives of the purpose of the Panchayati Raj system;
7. Appointing an Ombudsman to prevent corruption and punishment of the guilty;
8. Convincing the people of the importance of the Ward Sabhas and motivating officers to give proper guidance. Local Taluk Panchayat and Zilla Panchayat members, legislators and Parliamentarians to be present and give proper suggestions;

9. Legislators should whole-heartedly accept and support the administration by the Panchayati Raj Institutions and the principle of decentralization. Legislators should understand the basic purpose of the Constitution; and
10. Unnecessary interference by the government should stop. The practice of issuing illegal circulars and orders should be ended. We should take care that we do not oppose the very legislation which we ourselves enacted.

The Task before the Finance Commission

I am heading the third State Finance Commission with two eminent members, Mahendra S. Kanthi, son of S.R. Kanthi, Former Chief Minister of Karnataka and an expert in the field of economics and T. Thimme Gowda, a retired IAS officer with vast experience in administration and local self-government, who also has a background in economics. Our main purpose is to strengthen the Village Panchayats and suggest ways for the government to give more autonomy to the local bodies. Financial autonomy means release of funds, without any conditions. Unconditional grants to the local bodies with trained technical personnel are the basic needs for the autonomy of the local bodies. The essence of decentralization is creating an environment of awareness and culture of education in Gram Sabha. In a democracy, citizens' rights come with responsibilities.

Creating an environment of awareness is a prerequisite for successful devolution of financial and political power in any society. At present the functions of the local bodies are identified by the government and funds are earmarked in the link documents. Even the technical personnel are appointed by the government to implement the works of the local bodies. This is clearly violation of the principles laid down in the Constitution. At the same time, it is also necessary to suggest ways and means to improve the financial condition of the local bodies and make them stand on their own legs. Local bodies must be able to mobilize their own resources and they must be allowed to prepare their own plans and appoint the functionaries and provide better quality of service to the people. This is the very essence of autonomy for the local self-government.

Enacting more laws is not the solution for good and efficient governance. The Roman historian Tactitus said: "*The more corrupt the republic, the more laws. Too many laws destroy the rule of law because individuals will not honour them*". Adam Smith in *The Wealth of Nations* advocated simple laws which ordinary citizens can understand and comply with. Local self-governments have already been burdened with too many statutory provisions, rules and regulations which are difficult to understand and follow by the Gram Sabha. Hence, I think it is very essential for the progress of the country to give more powers and autonomy to the local bodies. Only then can we say that we respect the Constitution. Only then will the concept of Gram Rajya become real and the dream of Ram Rajya of Mahatma Gandhi come true.

6

The Nation Defending Porcupine

U.R. Ananthamurthy

How wonderful was Mani Shankar Aiyar's speech and how well Shrineevasa Murthy has translated it. I was very happy to hear it. Leeladevi Prasad and Kodagi have spoken about the shortcomings of our Panchayati Raj system. Udasi knows what are the shortcomings. Mani Shankar Aiyar has neatly summarized all these shortcomings and has spoken of their relevance to the entire country.

I still remember the time when Abdul Nazir Sab asked for and got the portfolio of Rural Development. Two persons stood behind him. One was Ramakrishna Hegde and the other was J.H. Patel. All the legislators had complaints about the system. Hegde sent me and Prof. B.K. Chandrasekhar to West Bengal to see how the Panchayati Raj system was working there. We visited West Bengal and gave a report. Even in West Bengal, ruled by the Communist Party, the legislators were not happy with the Panchayati Raj system. Bureaucracy was also not happy, because the problem of power sharing existed even in West Bengal. Abdul Nazir Sab knew about the existence of this problem. Even then he opted for the system because of his commitment to the concept of the 'Four Pillar State'. In this concept, the Centre, the State government, the District administration and the Village local government body were the four pillars. Should any one of these entities claim that it is the sole pillar, the edifice would not stand.

Let us have Universalist thinking

I have a request to make to Mani Shankar Aiyar. We started off to make this country great, but slowly and gradually our thinking became cosmopolitan. We are more cosmopolitan in our thinking. Mahatma Gandhi, Nehru, Rajiv Gandhi and here, Nazir Sab had Universalist thinking. 'Universalist' means that everything should reach every person. But today, our dream is that if a few cities grow big, we will make progress, India will become a great nation. Even the educated, the knowledgeable, the bureaucrats and the politicians, all dream of such a nation. Unless this changes, the Panchayati Raj will never grow as a true system. We need Mahatma Gandhi's universalist thinking. Everyone should reach that thinking. Our entire thinking process is undergoing change. Mani Shankar Aiyar must face this danger even within his own party, because in every party there is such a thinking. If you want to prove that it is not true, that by building a few great cities we are building a great nation, you should exercise your powers. Ordinary people should exercise power.

Need for Shame in Politics

Whenever a new government comes, Panchayati Raj system gets a beating. Because there is so much corruption, as soon as money comes, every one thinks about how to divide it among themselves. If Panchayat representatives also learn this, then there will be no way out for the nation. This should not happen. If this is not to happen, then everyone should take care and see what is happening. I have a hope that if more women get involved in administration there will be less corruption. Because they know how to run a family, looking after the needs of different members, and they still have a sense of shame. We have lost all shyness in politics. Shy politicians have become rare. I always say this. As long as there is a sense of shame in us, politics will remain healthy.

Panchayati Raj system is a part of this concept of Four Pillar State. Now we do not even need a large army for our nation. Mahatma Gandhi had a concept that if all the villages become autonomous then our nation will be like a porcupine; it will have thorns all over its body so that nobody can injure it. So we need a porcupine kind of an image for India where every village is strong. I want this Panchayati Raj system to go in that direction.

SECTION II

Panchayati Raj in Karnataka

Yesterday, Today and Tomorrow

7

Panchayati Raj in Karnataka — Yesterday

C. Narayanaswamy

Many prominent persons have already laid bare before you the concept of Panchayati Raj. Our national leaders extensively discussed in the presence of Mahatma Gandhi, as to what kind of administration we should have once we attain our freedom. Earlier there was a programme called the National Extension Programme. After independence we had development blocks. There were Block Development Officers. At that time, many central and State sponsored schemes were started and were implemented with a view to develop the rural areas. But development of rural areas is not possible only with the bureaucracy. It is possible only through the local people. Then a thinking started that we should establish an administrative system which involved people's representatives. A centralized administration is not feasible for India which has lakhs of villages. Centralized plan formulation is also not feasible. Power has to be decentralized. Plan formulation has to be decentralized. Administration has to be decentralized. With these objects in view the experiment of Panchayati Raj started.

Mahatma Gandhi did not want only the decentralization of power. He wanted that India should be a republic of villages. That is why, when the directive principles of State policy were incorporated in our Constitution, one of them said that the State should establish Gram Panchayats. There are three lists of subjects in our Constitution about what kind of administrative relationship should be there between the Centre and the States. One list concerns the Central government. Another list called the 'State List' concerns the State governments. The third is the concurrent list on which both the Centre and the States can legislate. According to these lists, the subject of Panchayati Raj falls within the State List. The Central Government cannot interfere in that. The respective State legislatures have to enact their own laws regarding the Panchayati Raj system.

Then why was the Constitution amended? Everyone accepted that the Panchayati Raj system should be established all over the country. The Central Government appointed a committee under the chairmanship of Balwant Rai Mehta to report on what should be the structure of this system. The report was sent to the States. Immediately after independence, many States tried with a lot of enthusiasm to make Bapu's dream come true. Several States appointed their own commissions. After independence, the then Mysore State and the present Karnataka State appointed Venkatappa Committee, Chandrasekharaiah Committee, etc. However, we remember the Kondajji Basappa Committee most.

Between 1987 and 1992, for five years, the Zilla Parishad and Mandal Panchayat system existed. We had followed the Asoka Mehta Committee in creating this system. In this four pillar State, the Centre, the State, the District and the Mandal were the four pillars. But in many States elections were not conducted for decades and administrators were appointed. Rural development was entrusted to the centralized direction and control of the State administration. The term 'Panchayati Raj' became a matter of ridicule. The representatives of the people had no place.

In States which had a government which believed in a decentralized system and in the Panchayati Raj system, a very good model of democratic decentralization came into being. There a new baby could be born. Wherever there was a lack of political will in such States the system wore out. There only a skeleton of a baby remained. When a government believing in democratic decentralization came to power, it would fill blood and flesh into the skeleton. In its absence the baby remained a skeleton. If this kind of a situation had to be put to an end, it was necessary to amend the Constitution and make the Panchayati Raj system mandatory. There was a need to create a system which did not depend on the fancies of the State governments, and which got its power straight from the Constitution.

The Earlier Efforts at Panchayati Raj

Earlier also there were progressive Panchayati Raj systems in some States. But making only the law, the rules, etc., does not amount to giving of power. The will power of the ruling governments becomes very important. For example, in West Bengal, the government changed in 1978. The Communists, who are till today in control, assumed power under the leadership of Jyoti Basu. They brought amendments to the existing Panchayati Raj Act and continued the system. Till today every five years they have conducted elections to the Panchayati Raj institutions. They also have a three-tier system.

Inspired by this State level experiment, an effort started at the national level. The first Zilla Panchayat to be established was in Nagaur district of Rajasthan. Karnataka has also earned a good name. To ensure social justice, a policy of reservation was implemented in Karnataka. In the 1960s this system was implemented in different States in different ways to suit local requirements. In Karnataka the Village Panchayats and Local Boards Act of 1959 came into force.

According to that Act, Gram Panchayats were established and elections were held. At the taluk level, the Taluk Development Boards were constituted. At the district level, District Development Boards under the chairmanship of the Deputy Commissioners were established. But these were not fully elected bodies. They had ex-officio members and officers.

Now, because of the Panchayati Raj system that was developed in Karnataka, the name of Abdul Nazir Sab occupies a permanent niche in our minds. His concept, his dream was to fulfil Mahatma Gandhi's vision of *Gram Rajya*. It was not only establishing Panchayats, but endowing them with necessary powers and programmes so as to enable them to function as units of local self-government.

The Karnataka Initiative

In Karnataka, a government under the leadership of Ramakrishna Hegde came to power in 1983. Then Abdul Nazir Sab took on the mantle of Rural Development and Panchayati Raj Minister. In the same year, he introduced the Zilla Parishads, Mandal Panchayats and Nyaya Panchayats Bill. It came up for discussion in the State Assembly and was entrusted to a joint select committee of the legislature. Abdul Nazir Sab took a delegation of leaders of all parties on a tour of different States of the country. Particular focus was laid on examining local self-government in West Bengal, Maharashtra and Gujarat. The delegates travelled extensively in West Bengal for many days. But the assent of the President of India for the Bill was delayed. Abdul Nazir Sab had to even threaten that he will fast until death in front of the Rashtrapati Bhavan. Ultimately, in 1985 the assent was given. Elections were held in January 1987. Since some persons approached a court of law, in some districts the elections had to be postponed. Except for Bangalore City, elections were held in all the remaining 19 districts.

I wish to tell you one thing in this connection. There is an ongoing discussion on the role of legislators and Parliament members in Panchayati Raj institutions. In 1983, the same question came up for discussion in the Karnataka legislature. If there are going to be only Zilla Parishads and Mandal Panchayats, what place will the legislators have? Legislators are also elected by the people. In the same areas they also have to shoulder the responsibility of development work. Hence, it was discussed as to how to accommodate them in the system. Ultimately, as a solution, an intermediate level institution called the Taluk Panchayat Samiti was created. The legislator of that area or the legislator who represented a large portion of the area of the taluk was made the ex-officio chairman. The Pradhans of the Mandal Panchayats in the Taluk, the Zilla Parishad members elected from the taluk, the President of the Cooperative Marketing Society, the President of the Land Development Bank in the Taluk were made the ex-officio members. There was no reservation like at present. The Taluk Panchayat Samiti itself had to co-opt, in all 5 members, including women and other backward class members.

The Constitutional Amendment

Prime Minister Rajiv Gandhi thought that rural development is possible only through decentralization of power. He used to freely praise the Panchayati Raj system put in place by parties opposed to him, the Janata Party in Karnataka and the Left parties in West Bengal. He used to ask why this system should not be established all over the country. The 64th amendment to the Constitution was introduced during his tenure. It received an overwhelming majority support in the Lok Sabha. In Rajya Sabha it was defeated merely by one vote. In 1989, V.P. Singh assumed office as the Prime Minister. His government also introduced a constitutional amendment bill. He had introduced a single bill covering both the rural and urban local bodies. But before it could be taken for discussion, the government fell. Thereafter, in 1991, P.V. Narasimha Rao became the Prime Minister. He continued the work of Rajiv Gandhi. With a view to realize the dream of Mahatma Gandhi of *Gram Rajya* he also introduced a constitutional amendment bill. A Joint Select Committee of the Parliament was constituted under the chairmanship of Ram Nivas Mirdha. When I was the President of a Zilla Parishad, I had received a questionnaire from the Joint Select Committee. I had sent my comments also.

Karnataka Act after the Amendment

After the coming into force of the constitutional amendment, Karnataka was the first State to enact a new Panchayati Raj Act. In accordance with the 1993 Panchayati Raj Act, in December of the same year, elections were held for the Gram Panchayats. Many people ask why the earlier system of Zilla Parishads and Mandal Panchayats was not revived. Some mandatory provisions have been added in the Constitution. If the population of a State is more than 5 lakh, then according to the Constitution, there has to be a three-tier Panchayati Raj system. Hence, it is not possible for us to have a two-tier system. The Constitution says that for the Panchayati Raj institutions also there should be a five-year term like those of the Parliament and the State Assemblies. Before the term of 5 years expires, elections have to be held to reconstitute new Panchayati Raj institutions. But we have interpreted this to mean that after the term of 5 years is over, we have to hold elections within the next 6 months.

Many States including Karnataka have thought like this. All parties think like this. There are many examples for this in our country. Many States have not held elections to these bodies in time and have postponed elections giving several reasons. If a Panchayat is dismissed for any reason before the end of the 5-year term, then for the remaining period an administrator can be appointed. So when any State, including Karnataka, postpones elections, it is a violation of the provisions of the Constitution.

Karnataka Panchayati Raj Act was drafted following the model of the West Bengal Act. There was a provision for Gram Sabhas and for the State Finance Commission. If you see the list of subjects entrusted to the Zilla Parishads, you will know that most of these subjects have now been entrusted to the Panchayati Raj institutions in the schedule to the constitutional amendment. This should make us proud. We may have been elected as candidates of any party, we may have been the active members of any party, but once we come to the Panchayati Raj institutions we should think that we belong to the Panchayat Party, we belong to the Panchayat caste. Otherwise it will become difficult to take the system forward.

The Question of Reservation

The question of reservation has also been discussed here. Under the Constitution it is mandatory to give reservation to the Scheduled Castes and Scheduled Tribes in accordance with their population in all three tiers. Women have to be given reservation of not less than one-third of seats. It is not mandatory under the Constitution to give reservation to the other backward classes. But the Constitution does not come in the way of giving reservation to them should any State legislature so wish. Accordingly, in the 1993 enactment, reservation has been provided for them. It became a little controversial in the Gram Panchayats. 'Backward' was defined as any person belonging to any caste or class whose annual income was less than Rs. 10,000 and who could get a certificate to that effect from the Tahsildar. Hence any person who could get such a certificate could contest elections from the seats reserved for the other backward classes. But this was set right later.

The Constitution does not say that legislators and members of Parliament should be given ex-officio membership. But should a State legislature so desire, it can give them the ex-officio membership in the district and the intermediate level panchayats. But since it is the legislators who make the law, in most of the States, they have provided the membership for themselves in the enactments.

As mentioned in the earlier session, it is true that the reservation for a period of 5 years is not enough for developing leadership. Rotation of reservation has been interpreted to mean changing of reservation after every term. But now Tamil Nadu has made it for two terms. We must welcome this. In the last elections to the Tamil Nadu assembly, i.e., before Ms. Jayalalitha became the Chief Minister, the representatives of the local bodies met her and told her that if she gives reservation for two terms then they will all support her in the Assembly elections. This was the reason for the amendment.

Distribution of Powers

There is still confusion as to who should do what at the village level, at the taluk level and at the district level. Our misfortune is that we have still not fully understood as to what is the scope of functions, what are the responsibilities, etc., of the elected representatives of these five tiers of Gram Panchayat, Taluk Panchayat, Zilla Panchayat, Assembly and the Parliament. When one tries to snatch the responsibility of another the confusion starts. But the intention of the Constitution is that the administration should be good, development works must be well done. One person cannot take on all the responsibilities. It should be distributed at various levels. We cannot say that we will totally ignore the legislators or members of Parliament because we need their help and cooperation for implementing the centrally sponsored and State sponsored schemes. We have to cooperate with each other and function within our jurisdictions.

Ramakrishna Hegde had published a book titled *District Government and Decentralized Administration*. I still have a copy of it. District local bodies have to grow as governments. This does not mean that they should make laws also. It means that they should fulfil the local requirements. They should have the power to mobilize resources. They should have their own programmes and should have staff with total control over them. Not only the entire country, but the entire world was observing our revolutionary experiment. I remember a team of researchers had come from the Oxford University then to study the system.

It is stated in the Constitution that women should be given not less than one-third reservation. In some places where there is no reservation, some women have contested against men and got elected. We have to welcome this. When we say not less than one-third, and if there is only one seat reserved for Scheduled Tribes, then it has to be given to a woman. For example, in all the five taluks of the Bangalore Rural District, one seat was reserved for Scheduled Tribes in each of the taluks and hence all these five seats had to be given to women belonging to the Scheduled Tribes. It is for this reason also that more women have been elected than the one-third envisaged in the Constitution. So far as Karnataka is concerned, we gave reservation to women to the extent of 25 per cent in the earlier enactment and this has helped in developing leadership among women. The women who were active in the Panchayati Raj institutions in those days could contest the elections to the legislative assembly.

Three Indicators of Success

Three points become very important to measure the success of any system: (1) What programmes have been given to them; (2) What funds have been devolved to them; and (3) What administrative staff have been provided to them. Earlier the Zilla Parishads had the power to appoint C and D grade employees. In many districts these appointments were made. But in the 1993, enactment it has been very clearly stated that the Panchayati Raj institutions have no power to appoint any staff. All of them will be government employees. The State government will have all the powers to transfer them from one district to another, from one taluk to another. Like the Public Service Commissions, there should be a separate commission for appointing the staff of the Panchayati Raj institutions. In Andhra Pradesh there is such a commission. They have provided for the appointment and transfer and for formulation of their service conditions. There is scope for this in our Act also. But our State has not done this so far. Earlier the Zilla Parishad had the power to appoint the Secretary to the Mandal Panchayat after consulting it. Now they are appointing whomsoever they want. We are all parties to it. We are all benefiting from it in one way or the other.

We have made so much progress in our State. When we look back, we see that still there are so many shortcomings. Yet we are still different from other States. We have travelled farther. If those holding power work honestly, even the bureaucracy will cooperate. We should respect each other and work together. Let us discuss how to acieve this during the next two days. Thank you !

8

Panchayati Raj in Karnataka — Today

Savita Ramesh

Whatever we have experienced in the past with regard to Panchayati Raj is an old time dream of Mahatma Gandhi. The Panchayati Raj that we are experiencing today is in a pathetic condition. This is my feeling. I have worked as the Vice President of a Zilla Panchayat for ten months. The first problem I encountered was with regard to the powers. What are the powers of the President and the Vice President of the Zilla Panchayat? What are their privileges? How can they take the district on the path of development in the best way possible? Today, the Presidents and Vice Presidents of the Zilla Panchayats are limited to the role of getting garlanded, honoured and praised in functions. Because they are not in a position to give specific answers to any questions relating to the problems of the district. Section 193 of the 1993 Act says that the President of the Zilla Panchayat is the executive head. But nowhere have his powers, privileges, or responsibilities, etc., been clearly defined. In the Act of 1983, all these were clearly defined. In addition, they were also given the status of a Minister of State. For these reasons, they could take the districts on the path of development.

In the same way, if an officer was undisciplined, there was some control over him. Today, even if an officer commits indiscipline, the President or the Vice President cannot take any action against him. If a complaint is lodged, a departmental enquiry will be conducted against him. At the time of enquiry, some influential person will interfere and all his mistakes will be covered up. He would be saved by transferring him to some other place or by doing something else. Hence it is not possible for us to keep the officers and the staff of the Zilla Panchayats under our control. In the earlier system, I understand that the President could take action even against the Chief Secretary of the Zilla Parishad who was a senior IAS officer.

The Powerless Presidents

Today we are unable to take action against even an ordinary employee. We cannot even transfer him. We cannot appoint them also. For example, in Chikmagalur district, in all the departments put together, 2,089 posts are vacant. Under such circumstances, how can the President or the Vice President carry out any work in any of the departments in the absence of staff? In most of the schools established for the poor students, the most rotten quality of foodgrains are being supplied. There is cheating in attendance of teaching staff. When a member from the area or the President or the Vice President pays a visit to make an enquiry, you will not find any supervisor there. You only get the poor cook. You cannot take any action against the cook. When we enquire as to where is the supervisor, the answer is that since he has two more hostels to supervise, he has gone to visit those hostels. When we go there, we are told that he has gone back. Hence, we are unable to check the stocks. We are unable to control anything. When this is discussed in the Zilla Panchayat meetings, the higher officers say that nothing can be done because the supervisor has been given the responsibility of three or four places. He might have gone there. As a result the food given to the poor students in the schools is of very poor quality.

The Problem of Teachers and Doctors

Another problem facing the representatives of rural areas is the problem of teachers in schools who always want to go away to the urban areas. When the month of March comes, they bring recommendations from the Chief Minister or some one else, and do not teach in schools till July or August. Only dealings take place, no teachings. There is a rule that the newly recruited school teachers should serve in rural areas for five years. After the mandatory five years they bring influence and return to cities. Again the posts in rural schools remain vacant.

I admit that even our legislators are representatives of the people. They also know about the shortage of teachers in the villages. So why should teachers be transferred to the places they prefer to go to? If that goes on happening, I think it is better to close all government schools. Legislators are not easily accessible to the ordinary people. The members of the Gram Panchayats, Taluk Panchayats and Zilla Panchayats have to pass in front of the schools almost every day. When we see the animosity on the face of the villagers when they pass by us, we feel ashamed. We feel that we should not have become members of the Panchayati Raj institutions because we have no powers. We can neither appoint teachers nor transfer them. In cities, if there are 5 posts of teachers, 6 of them will be working there. There is no provision under which the additional teacher at least can be transferred to the rural areas. Even if a teacher in a city is suspended, he has to be transferred to places only 3 to 4 kilometres away only and cannot be transferred to the rural areas. These are all very serious problems.

There is also a problem of doctors, who also do not want to serve in rural areas. We give training to nurses through the Zilla Panchayats. Even there, the ANMs do not want to serve in rural areas. If training is given to the locals, then they will work in the villages. But then the circulars by the government do not permit this. We have to see marks obtained, etc., and give training to a nurse who comes from a different area. Such a person will get trained and go back to his or her place and not serve in our villages. Hence, while giving this type of trainings, we should give priority to the local candidates. This will certainly improve the position with regard to ANMs.

The Interference by the Government

Another important problem in this connection is that for everything there is a government directive. If government goes on giving directions on everything how can the Zilla Panchayats function independently? If the government wants to keep control over finances, let them do so by issuing circulars. But I strongly feel that the government should reduce the number of circulars being issued to the PRIs. We are now giving a lot of funds to the Gram Panchayats. But in Gram Panchayats bill collectors or watermen have been made the secretaries. It is not possible for them to spend such funds. They also cannot understand the law. Hence, it is necessary that an experienced person of the Rural Development and Panchayati Raj department is appointed as the Secretary of the Gram Panchayat.

Shortage of Staff

More than all this, nearly 7 to 8 villages come within the jurisdiction of one Zilla Panchayat member. One Zilla Panchayat member gets one junior engineer. It is not possible for him to prepare the estimates for the action plans of these 7 to 8 Gram Panchayats. Because in Gram Panchayats there are many works worth Rs. 10,000. Thus even engineers are not available to us because they will have to serve 7 to 8 Gram Panchayats. Whenever we ask them as to where they were, the stock answer is that they were in another panchayat. So it is necessary to increase the number of engineers and to reduce their burden.

Give us the Funds

Within the funds allotted to the Zilla Panchayats we prepare ordinary action plans and go on implementing them. But the funds given for drought or floods are not given to the Zilla Panchayats but to the Deputy Commissioners. By the time the drought or floods come, our action plans would be over. If drought or floods come after that, people only notice what the Zilla Panchayat does. Whatever the problem, they first think of Zilla Panchayats. They protest in front of the Zilla Panchayat office. But it is not possible for us to respond to their problems. When the drought or floods action plan is prepared, the members of the Zilla Panchayat are not involved in it. Only the legislators and Deputy Commissioner prepare them.

However, sometimes, when people protest, the Chief Executive Officer of the Zilla Panchayat, because of pressure from the MLA or some others, includes some works under the engineering division. But when the action plan is prepared by the MLA and the Deputy Commissioner, this work is not included in it. Then from where should we find funds for it? This becomes a big problem for the Zilla Panchayats. Since the action plan is implemented elsewhere, it is possible that the work carried out by the Zilla Panchayat is included in the action plan resulting in double billing. This may not come to the knowledge of the Zilla Panchayat members also. Even the MLAs may not come to know about it. Thus there is direct interference by the MLAs and the Deputy Commissioners in the working of the Zilla Panchayats. Both the Zilla Panchayat members and the MLAs are elected representatives of the people. It is absolutely necessary that both of us work together for the all-round development of the district. Because of this kind of confusion, misunderstanding crops up between us. This only results in problems and not in the development of the district. Instead of this, all the funds earmarked for the Zilla Panchayats should be directly given to the Zilla Panchayats. Only then will proper development of the district be possible.

The Finance Commission Recommendations

Another big problem faced by the Zilla Panchayats concerns the recommendations of the twelfth Finance Commission.

According to those, we have to prepare the action plans. But the legislators bring pressure on the government and get circular after circular issued and create confusion. I am one of the victims of such confusion. One day when a general meeting was in progress, the legislator from my area told his followers that he had brought money from the government but the Zilla Panchayat was not sanctioning it. As a result his followers entered the meeting and created problems. Do they not have any confidence in the Panchayati Raj system? The legislators should make laws and not create problems by getting circulars issued. I request them not to create this kind of crisis for us.

The Finance Commission has recommended the grant of funds to the Panchayati Raj Institutions. But the government is not giving the recommended amounts to the PRIs. This is against the Constitution. If the funds recommended by the Finance Commission are given to us, we can decide on the priorities and prepare our budgets and carry on our work independently.

According to Section 256 of the 1993 Act, the *Finance, Audit and Planning Committee* of the Zilla Panchayat has to prepare the annual budget and get it approved by the general meeting of the Zilla Panchayat. But there are some problems here. When the Zilla Panchayat prepares its annual budget and sends it to the government, the budget undergoes change at the government level. As a result of this, the Panchayats have become mere dolls and are unable to function independently. Hence all the money required for the plans should be released according to the needs and the reality as perceived at the local level. The Government should not alter or change the budgets prepared by the Zilla Panchayats. Just as the Zilla Panchayat Presidents and Vice Presidents were invited to meetings to discuss the State Plans in the Planning Department of the Government prior to 1983, they should be invited now too. When what is required in our district is discussed in our presence it becomes possible for us get what we want done.

In 2003, there used to be a considerable amount left over as the closing balance in the Zilla Panchayats. Hence, there was no dearth of money to carry on the works in accordance with the annual budget. But now, the money not spent before 31st March, has to be returned to the Government. They release the money by 20th March and expect us to spend it by the 30th ! Let the government keep control so that the money is not misused. But do they have no confidence in the grass root level institutions? If not, let them keep everything to themselves.

There may be a problem facing one district which may not be a problem in another district. But you people sitting here in the State capital, give the same amount of money to the health sector in all the districts. For instance, in Chikmagalur district we have a *monkey fever.* It is not found in other districts. So it is better to fix an amount for the health sector and send it to us, so that the Zilla Panchayat can decide how much money is required for which health programme. Previously the health department had constructed several buildings. Most of them have become dilapidated. Money should be released to get them repaired. We will get only such buildings repaired which are necessary for us or else we will spend the money on buying medicines. Hence it is necessary to send us untied funds.

Gram Panchayats can levy taxes and mobilize resources. But the Zilla Panchayats do not have that power. If the State legislature so desires, it can empower all the three tiers of the Panchayati Raj Institutions to levy taxes, fees, etc., and mobilize their resources. But the income received by the Zilla Panchayats from horticulture, agriculture, social forestry, fishery, etc., has to be deposited with the State government. The Panchayats should be allowed to retain and use these monies. Necessary amendments should be brought to the Act to enable this.

Give us Freedom, we will fulfil Gandhi's Dream.

Instead of giving us only guidelines, let the State

Government give us more freedom. We have a feeling that the earlier system was better. If you give more autonomy and more responsibilities to the Panchayati Raj institutions they will certainly be able to function better and realize the dream of Mahatma Gandhi.

9

Panchayati Raj in Karnataka — Tomorrow

Geeta Sethi

My vision for panchayats is what I have learnt from all of you. It is your vision. Here, I am just stating your vision. India opted for decentralization to increase the accountability of government, to reach out to rural people and to improve services and expenditures. It is about people getting involved in governance.

Decentralization is about moving governments closer to people by giving them a say in budget formation that better reflects their priorities. It is about nation building. Over 70 per cent of the people are still in rural areas. Urbanization will take time, till then we need to show that the economic advantages of the country's eight per cent growth rate is trickling down to rural India.

The Central Government seized on this opportunity first with the central schemes, where vertical programmes were designed to involve rural people in governance and nation building. Then came the Constitution Amendments which mandated rural and urban decentralization along with political decentralization (holdling of periodic local body elections) and also tried to provide some autonomy in the form of taxing powers. The constitutional amendments also mandated the creation of State Finance Commissions to tell States how to get their houses in order to strengthen local governments by providing for a hospitable inter-governmental fiscal system.

Despite very difficult conditions and no support, it is amazing what some panchayats have been able to achieve. In Karnataka, for example, the own-source revenues in some of the Gram Panchayats have increased ten-fold. And we know people are only willing to pay if they are receiving services that seem important to them — health services that the Kerala panchayats have been providing despite absenteeism in health workers of around 30 per cent, financed by their own budgets. And in West Bengal, the only reason schools are operating in almost all of the rural areas is because of the initiative of Gram Panchayats to hire *para* (neighbourhood) teachers. Publications and the literature are full of such stories where panchayats despite very difficult circumstances are still being able to provide services to improve the lives of rural constituents. But the question is, why do we have such a difficult landscape for panchayats to deliver and get empowered? Why is there resistance from higher level government, why are we suspicious of their intention and their capacity?

The Resistance by States

What can we say has happened so far with respect to decentralization in India? The States have resisted mightily. The allocation to local governments in Kerala, Karnataka, West Bengal is on an average between 20-25 per cent of State expenditures only. Moreover, the State Finance Commissions have really not been effective. And even where there are more reasonable inter-governmental transfer systems (as in Kerala), the transfers may have been under-funded because of the fiscal incapacity of the State. As a result, Gram Panchayats underperform and the Gram Sabha is inactive. What seems interesting is that whatever strength Panchayati Raj institutions have been given is largely due to Centrally Sponsored Schemes. Though they do not provide much autonomy, they do account for a significant part of revenues and these resources may be equalizing (as seen in West

Bengal, where poor panchayats get more money from these central schemes).

So what is wrong? The State fiscal situation is in a mess, hence they are in no position to share their revenue base with the local governments. State deficits for Kerala, Karnataka and West Bengal are high. The messy State fiscal position is due in part to a flawed system of inter-governmental fiscal relations between the Centre and the States and in part due to the fiscal indiscipline at the State level. Further, panchayats do not have the capacity to absorb service responsibility or taxing power. The States have not devolved enough power because the State bureaucracy is unwilling to yield. And furthermore, States do not even have enough information to evaluate the finances of panchayats.

The question, then, is what can be done? The current administration at the Centre sees rural governments as the key mechanism for delivering key services to rural people and one of its priorities is to make this approach work in some States to serve as an example and a model for the rest of the country. Karnataka is such an example, a State that has taken on this challenge and requested the World Bank to partner with them. They wanted to know what has worked in other countries, and what has not. And they wanted the design of the successful stories around the world to get reflected in the design in Karnataka, without violating the strengths of the local democracy and the legal framework. And now Karnataka is well on its way in working out this vision into reality.

Karnataka—The Ideal Ground

Karnataka is the ideal candidate for a model of decentralized service delivery to set an example for the rest of India. The poorest parts of Karnataka have many features typical of more northern States, with high incidence of poverty, difficult access and service resource constraints. But Karnataka also has a long history of rural local governments — more than any other State in India. For many years it was a pioneer in sub-State devolution. Its 1983 reforms served as the basis of the constitutional amendments. It is now regaining leadership in this agenda through some bold steps. Karnataka realized that the challenge is at the State level. The State government realized it has to provide enough resources with functions that are important to rural citizens and begin to look at the panchayats for delivery of such services. Karnataka also realized that it is extremely important and very crucial that State Finance Commissions are made functional by upgrading the data and providing support to analytic cells to do the work. It also realized that they needed to raise the tax effort to support panchayat financing.

The transfers from the Centre and State need to be more untied than they are right now, thereby giving Panchayati Raj institutions more autonomy so that they are able to provide services to rural constituents. But at the same time capacity upgrading at the panchayats has to take place. Redirecting of line department expenditures towards the Panchayati Raj institutions has to take place once capacity is upgraded. And finally, the Urban Local Bodies have to mobilize more revenues and the State needs to begin moving them off the grant system, so that more grant support is available for rural local governments.

The Partnership Programme

So what is this partnership programme that is helping realize the vision for new Panchayati Raj in the State of Karnataka? This is the first local government operation in South Asia that is providing institutional and policy strengthening. It is a $120 million loan for five years. The development objective of the programme is to improve effectiveness of service delivery by Karnataka's Gram Panchayats, particularly with respect to the management of public resources and the delivery of relevant services that the rural people prioritize.

The project will be considered satisfactory if the following outcomes are achieved :

- Raising the number of meetings of the Gram Sabhas with high representative participation and relevant participatory plans to reflect community preferences of local population;
- Rising satisfaction of village residents with service delivery by Gram Panchayats;
- Gradual increase in own-source revenue and stronger financial health of Gram Panchayats.

Karnataka said, we need a reform in the transfer system, we want the transfer system to be predictable, we want it to be equalizing, we want it to be transparent. So the first big component is the transfer system. The allocation of resources to the poorest 39 taluks is large enough so that panchayats can look meaningful; it is equalizing—weightage is given to needs—population, percentage of agricultural wage labourers, and percentage of Scheduled Castes and Scheduled Tribes, and rewards are given for improved own revenues. The expenditure decisions are through a participatory manner that will be monitored, to be a better reflection of what the rural constituents want.

The second big component is capacity building. This is at three levels: at the State level in terms of having basic information on both fiscal and non-fiscal variables that allow the State to carry out inter-governmental policies sub-nationally; and hoping this new information that is being collected for the first time in Karnataka for all the panchayats will provide the first ever glimpse of what the expenditures and revenues are, what the fiscal picture at the panchayat looks like. This information will also help the State Finance Commissions to provide recommendations that are more meaningful for the State.

The next level capacity building is at the panchayat level—basic training, building capacity on making budgets, financial management, planning, etc.

And the third level of capacity building is at the constituents' level. What are their rights and roles in the decision making process at the panchayat level? Where should they go if they have a grievance, etc.

World Bank and Decentralization

Although keeping a low profile, the World Bank has been a big supporter of decentralization in India. This is the new Bank that President Wolfensen created, a Bank that cares about people and the poor. For the last six years, the World Bank has provided unconditional support to the decentralization agenda at the Central and State levels, in particular to Karnataka, Kerala, and West Bengal, through studies, knowledge forums and projects. In addition, the Bank also supported the creation of an association of panchayats all over India.

This programme of the State is really about institutionalizing many of its processes to improve decision making at the lowest level. It is about recognizing that panchayats are an integral part of the inter-governmental structure in India. All of this leads towards realizing the vision of the new panchayats in Karnataka.

10

Two Steps Forward, One Step Backward

The Practical Path to Progress

M.P. Prakash

Savita Ramesh is the best example to demonstrate the kind of leadership that can develop when responsibility is entrusted to the grass root levels. If you can learn about the law, about your responsibilities, about your duties, about how to carry on your work, it would be a great contribution to the empowerment of women. When change has to be brought about, it is not as easy as you perhaps think. Whenever a society takes to the path of progress, on issues of self-governance, and develops its philosophy, its struggles, you will have two options. The first is bringing about change through bullets, through bloodshed, through violence. The second option is by getting power through the ballot box in a democratic system. This struggle for democracy has deep roots. It is precisely to look at the factors that strengthen these roots, that nurture them, that this discussion on *Panchayati Raj – Yesterday, Today and Tomorrow* has been organized. How was it earlier? What has happened today? What should happen tomorrow? You should discuss these in a practical way in the light of your experiences. What kind of a system do we desire? Are we ready for it, do we have the necessary mental make-up for it?

Winston Churchill used to say, *"this poor country which has hundreds of languages, thousands of castes, which has unhealthy, uncivilized people who have no economic security, is incapable of democratically governing itself. That is why I will not give it freedom"*. But Mahatma Gandhi said, *"instead of people who are six thousand miles away governing me, let my nearer ones govern me. I do not want a good government, I want self-government"*. How far are we ready for this self-government today? How far are the members of the Zilla Panchayat ready to share their experiences, their capabilities, and their cooperation with the members of the Taluk Panchayat? In the same way, how far are the members of the Taluk Panchayat ready to share power with the Gram Panchayats? What is the attitude of the Gram Panchayat members towards strengthening of Gram Sabhas? If you think on these lines, you will know that in our hearts we all lean towards centralized systems.

Resistance to Sharing Power

When Devegouda became the Chief Minister in 1994, 68 legislators, including the one who was a Minister of State under the harbinger of the Panchayati Raj system, Abdul Nazir Sab, gave a memorandum in writing that it was not necessary to hold panchayat elections and that schemes like 'Ashraya' need not be given to the panchayats, and that development is possible only when it is under the control of the legislators. This means that even those who talk of decentralization are not mentally ready to share power with others. We are your elder brothers sitting here in the Assembly. Our elder brothers are sitting in the Parliament. You are our younger brothers sitting in the Zilla panchayat. Those younger to you are sitting in the Taluk Panchayats. Youngest are sitting in the Gram Panchayats. We should not try to sacrifice an ideology by showing some defects in administration. Here somebody is taking Rs. 2,000 as bribe for Ashraya house, the work is not being done properly. All this is wrong. These are administrative lapses known to all. But these lapses should not shake our commitment to an ideology. What do they say in the Assembly? *We have to ask the Zilla Panchayat members even for a drinking water well. In that case why should we be MLAs?*

What is your job? What is their job? How should the grass root level democracy be? What should be our mental make-up for that? I was looking into a book just now. S.K. Dey promoted the concept of community development. I understand that Jawaharlal Nehru visited his training centre. He felt that all the money there was going down the drain and that these people will never get any training. But when he returned to Delhi he said about S.K. Dey, *he is a mad fellow. But give him whatever money he asks. I know that all that money will go down the drain. He will not be able to do anything. Even then, give him the money.*

The Inspiration for Amending the Constitution

Ramakrishna Hegde had organized a huge rally of more than 80,000 people who had got elected for the first time after the implementation of the Panchayati Raj Act, in the Palace grounds in Bangalore. Narasimha Rao had come. S.K. Dey had also come. Influenced by this, Narasimha Rao carried forward the dream of Rajiv Gandhi of establishing the Panchayati Raj system in the entire country. When Asoka Mehta was preparing his report on the Panchayati Raj system, some prominent citizens had demanded that a constitutional amendment should be brought to provide for the Panchayati Raj system. Among those prominent citizens were Ramakrishna Hegde, S.M. Joshi, Madhu Limaye, etc. But as the Janata Government fell the constitutional amendment could not be brought. If you go back to 1947, in the draft constitution there was not even a reference to Panchayati Raj. Dr. Ambedkar said that the *villages are dens of casteism*. Exploiters, upper caste people, English knowing people were ruling in the villages.

Panchayats in Karnataka

We also had a three-tier democratic system. The Kondajji Basappa Committee had said that the system was not working well and wanted more powers to be given to it. In

1964, Ramakrishna Hegde had moved a bill based on these recommendations. It was nothing compared to the present Act. It was a toothless Bill which did not give any powers to you. Even such a Bill was defeated in the legislature by a mere 3 votes' difference. Ramakrishna Hegde resigned. The then Chief Minister Nijalingappa did not accept the resignation but made him the Minister for Finance and Excise. This was a blessing in disguise which is a different story.

But since Hegde had kept this in mind, when he became the Chief Minister in 1983, he chose a person like Abdul Nazir Sab who had a commitment to the cause of Panchayati Raj and entrusted the job of creating Zilla Parishads, Mandal Panchayats and Nyaya Panchayats to him. It took two years for the Bill to get the assent of the President of India. The assent was given after Abdul Nazir Sab threatened that he would fast till death in front of the Rashtrapati Bhavan unless the assent was given. Then there were people committed to the cause of Panchayati Raj. There were people who had a sense of shame in public. They had a mind to do some service. Today we have given up all these values. You should introspect yourselves. You need not take us as role models.

The Social Resistance

Society does not accept immediate changes. It keeps going back to the values established in the past. In such circumstances, the people will question you. Elections are postponed. That means your powers have been curtailed. But which of you have passed any resolution against this in your Zilla Panchayats? We say, *we are the ones who give you tickets, we give the money, you should listen to what we say*. You talk very nicely when we are far, but do you talk in our presence? This is the reason for the present sad state of the Panchayati Raj.

Under such circumstances, we had to postpone the creation of Nyaya Panchayats for five years. When people like Mallikarjun Kharge were members of the Joint Select Committee, there was a very good concept of Nyaya Panchayats. That it should be elected by the Gram Panchayats only, that it should have 5 members, that women, scheduled castes and scheduled tribes and other backward class people must have compulsory representation. There should be two more persons from the general category. These five persons should have power to impose fines but not imprison. This power had to be exercised unanimously, and not like the Supreme Court where the judgement given by 6 judges is the judgement of the Court and the judgement given by 5 other judges is not the judgement at all. We had created these toothless Nyaya Panchayats with very limited powers, so that nobody was suppressed, nobody was exploited. After observing whether this experiment will succeed or not, we wanted to implement the whole scheme after five years. But what happened? The government fell.

The new government that came to power brought the Act of 1993. On the surface the Act was to comply with the Constitution 73rd Amendment but then there were many defects in the Act. So when we came to power, in order that the Act was not amended often, we brought about 63 amendments. With the help of officers like Shreenivasa Murthy, Meenakshisundaram and Satish Chandran, we amended the Act and gave powers to the Panchayati Raj institutions. But our system is such that nobody writes about Shreenivasa Murthy or others who did this commendable job.

There also we have a stratified system. Excuse me for talking like this. George Mathew, there are people who want to ignore the changes that we brought. They don't even mention those changes. Not that I want the name of Shreenivasa Murthy or any other person to be mentioned. But is it not history? Even your Institute of Social Sciences does not write about this. Even the intellectuals who write articles about Panchayati Raj do not mention this. You have to work in these circumstances.

The Right to Commit Mistakes

What has happened today? Your brethren who were trained have now become MLAs and Ministers. But all of us say that we want Ashraya. Indira Awas Scheme is of the Central Government. Hence, legislators are not the chairmen for those committees. Ashraya is a State Government scheme. Hence the legislators say that it is our money and hence we will become chairmen. They became the chairmen of those committees. Did you protest? Did you struggle? It is not all that easy. Balwantray Mehta had said, *"we have a right to commit mistakes"*. It is wrong to condemn you for having committed a mistake. That is why we have provided reservations for women, for backward classes, etc. We call it a 'legislative anomaly'.

According to the 1991 Census, about 7,000 seats were reserved for the Scheduled Tribes. In many Gram Panchayats only one seat was reserved for the STs. According to the Constitution, this seat had to be reserved for women belonging to the STs. Hence, of the 7,000 seats reserved for the STs more than 6,000 women got elected. Some legislators like Tippeswamy belonging to the STs told me, *"aren't there men in our communities, you have brought in 6,000 women from 7,000 seats reserved for STs. Please let men also speak about their problems"*. I said, *"you men have been talking about your problems for the past several years. Now let women talk about their problems"*.

The Need to Accommodate

I remember once what J.H. Patel jokingly told Ramakrishna Hegde, in a legislature party meeting: *Ramakrishna Hegde, you are 3,000 years old. S.R. Bommai, you are 800 years old. B. Rachaiah, you are only 50 years old.* What he meant was that the Brahmins were very forward because of 3,000 years of their civilization, culture, education, etc. Bommai, who was converted as Lingayat by Basavanna was 800 years old and hence the Brahmin should be liberal towards him. Bommai who was 800 years old, should be very liberal with Rachaiah who got self-confidence, self-respect, organization and struggle only after Ambedkar. You should all develop this kind of liberalism. We should not hang on to some mistake somewhere,repeating, *this thing happened in SC/ST Corporation, that thing happened in the Backward Class Corporation*. These things happen in any system. We should correct these mistakes. Do not think that we talk about this philosophy, this ideology in the assembly session. D.R. Patil is one person who struggles in the assembly. He is our only hope. Sharanaprakash Patil, who won for the first time from Sedam, also fights in the assembly. What a situation ! We should either be in power or out of it. This is the situation. Ideology also has to change on many occasions to suit the reality. We have to show that wisdom.

One young man was referring to the Employment Guarantee Scheme. This Scheme is implemented only in some districts like Shimoga, Chikmagalur, Kodagu, etc. Somehow Bellary has also been added. This is not implemented in Koppal, in Gagad. What is the yardstick of the Central Government to implement this scheme? They say that it should be implemented in districts where many farmers have committed suicides. Now we will have to go to other districts and say that more farmers should commit suicide so that the scheme could be implemented.

You should welcome the banning of liquor. D.R. Patil used to ask many questions on banning of liquor. You have the power to grant licenses to liquor shops. Even though the Excise Department auctions the marketing rights, you should say that the license must be obtained from the Gram Panchayat. In Gadag all Gram Panchayats together took a decision to ban liquor. In Sandur, Ghorpade persuaded all Gram Panchayats to take a similar decision. I came to know the secret later. Next to Sandur there is a police station at Gadignur of Hospet Taluk. It is not a very profitable police station. Even then many people were bringing pressure to get transferred to the Gadignur police station. When I enquired as to why people were particular about Gadignur, I came to know that liquor was being supplied to Sandur through Gadignur and hence the *mamul* was decided at the Gadignur police station. Because of the struggle by many persons, the Gram Panchayats could get the power to issue licenses to liquor shops. As a result of this you can cancel a license now. True, liquor will again come to your village. Instead of sachets it will come in bottles. That is a different thing. You should understand the system. In development, in reform, when we take two steps forward and one step backward, only then can we reach our goal. We cannot achieve our goals all at once. We cannot change the mindsets of all at once. We cannot establish the Ram Rajya all at once. When we establish it theoretically, experimentally, we will have to correct the mistakes in it.

We have now entrusted the responsibility of drinking water supply to the Zilla Panchayats. Because the Gram Panchayats are not capable of taking up the responsibility. In Teerthahalli taluk, the Gram Panchayats are efficiently managing the drinking water supply for the past many years. You were told to keep the toolkits but how many Gram Panchayats have kept them? When we were training people to repair bore wells we gave you money to send people to get the training. You did not bother about it. Tell me the truth ! Don't you distribute the grants received by the Gram Panchayat among yourselves? If I get Rs. 50,000 I get a drain constructed for that amount only. We let drain water run off in front of the house of the person we don't like in the village. Is this sort of thing not going on?

Mistakes That We Commit

And then you want to have all the contracts. What mistakes we are making! As we run around to get contracts for persons of our choice, you are also doing the same thing. Earlier it was not like this. Then we were afraid of what people would say. That is why we have introduced the concept of social audit. Socially there should be an audit of accounts. I had thought that you would be more afraid of the people than we were. Because we are far away from the people, our corruption, our nepotism would not be known to the people in the villages.

Sreenivasa Murthy has to give you today Rs. 800 crore. From where should he bring money to pay your electricity bills? Last time we paid Rs. 25 crore and gave you a clean slate. Don't you have the basic consciousness that once you are given a clean slate, thereafter you should pay your electricity bills? As soon as you get money you start contracts, getting mud roads constructed, getting mud drains constructed. You should grow beyond these things. Only then can Panchayati Raj, power sharing and democratic decentralization succeed.

Let Us Bring Changes, Even If Small Ones

In the background of all these views, the Rural Development and Panchayati Raj department of the Government of Karnataka and the Institute of Social Sciences of Dr. George Mathew have organized this convention. Dr. Mathew has tried to reach these ideas to many other States. Without his efforts, Ms. Geetha Sethi of the World Bank would not have evinced such an interest in Karnataka. He has worked in such a way that people from different spheres can understand the issues. He is also a crusader. He is fighting to bring about change. It is his another struggle like that of our Nazir Sab. We get elected with commitment to our party. But don't think that everyone thinks like us in our party. On many occasions, whether we like it or not, we also tend to become part of the system. But we should still try to bring about small changes in the system.

SECTION III

Special Session
Panchayati Raj:
Jammu & Kashmir, Karnataka

11

Panchayati Raj in Jammu & Kashmir

A Sad Story

Abdul Rahim Rather

Twenty years ago, on this day, Karnataka had initiated a new Panchayati Raj system. Today we have come together here to celebrate that day. We are very thankful to George Mathew and his colleagues for having given me this opportunity to be with you to celebrate the event, to evaluate the Panchayati Raj that was started here and to see what are the advantages of the system and what are its shortcomings. George Mathew and the Institute of Social Sciences are doing wonderful work in the field of democratic decentralization. We have to appreciate their efforts. Recently they organized a big conference *Indian Federalism at Work* at Srinagar and inspite of several difficulties they organized it in such a way that to us it became an event never to be forgotten.

Our Guide : Karnataka

It was in 1985 that in Srinagar, Farooq Abdulla, who has been Chief Minister of Kashmir for three times, told me and my colleagues that the Karnataka legislature has passed a revolutionary enactment on Panchayati Raj and that we should go there, study the enactment and its implementation, to what extent it was solving the problems of the people. We were then in the opposition, we were not in power. But we were carrying on an agitation for reviving the Panchayati Raj system. The government of the time had dissolved the panchayats and in the place of elected panchayats, it had nominated some persons, some committees which were carrying on the Panchayati Raj just for the name's sake. For three years we carried on our agitation but nothing happened.

Before this, in 1985 when we had come to Karnataka, we were told that the law had been passed but its implementation had not started, that it will take some time and that we should come back when it is implemented and see how it is being implemented. And then elections to the Assembly were held in 1987 and we again came to power. After coming to power, I and my two esteemed friends had come here. George Mathew was referring to this in his speech in the morning. Mohammed Shafi, who was the then Minister for Agriculture and Rural Development, Pyarelal Handu, who was the then Minister for Law and myself, the three of us had come here. We studied the Act, we held some discussions and after our return we prepared a new Panchayati Raj bill. We are thankful to the Institute of Social Sciences and particularly to George Mathew for helping us draft that bill. They brought several experts and conducted some seminars and some discussion in Kashmir on the subject.

In 1987, Karnataka was the first State which had enacted this new law, a revolutionary new law. Even in 1993, Karnataka was the first State to enact a new law and implement it. I have also heard that about two years ago a comprehensive amendment was made to this law to widen its scope and make it a better law. Through the amendments the Gram Sabhas have been given more powers, to make people's participation possible. And the frequency of meetings of the Gram Panchayats has been increased. Meetings of the Gram Panchayats which were being held once in two months, are now being held every month. You have also made it compulsory now that members of the Zilla Panchayat or the Taluk Panchayat have to declare their assets. In the same way, the money that is being spent on the elections will have to be disclosed by the contestants. And if there is anything wrong with the declaration the member may even be disqualified. This is just like the law which is applicable to the members of Parliament and Assemblies.

The Problem of Resources

I think that the major problem of the Panchayati Raj institutions all over the country is one of shortage of money, shortage of funds. It is a problem of finances. May be the position in Karnataka is better compared to other States. Even so, I think even here this kind of shortage is being felt. So far as schemes are concerned, that is, the Centrally Sponsored Schemes, the guidelines given are very tough. The money given to the Gram Panchayats is tied, i.e., it is mentioned as to where the money is to be spent. Hence the Gram Panchayats cannot take up any work for which there is more demand, which are more necessary.

In some of the States it is seen that the money received in the name of the panchayats is diverted and that money does not reach these institutions at all. One good thing is that the present Union Panchayati Raj ministry has formed a monitoring committee under the chairmanship of the Union Secretary for Panchayati Raj. The money sent from above, from the Finance Ministry, is monitored by this committee. Another good thing is the recommendation of the Twelfth Finance Commission that Rs. 20,000 crore be allotted to the Panchayati Raj institutions. This money is to be spent in five years between 2005 and 2010. May be these steps will to some extent solve the financial problems of the Panchayati Raj institutions.

The second suggestion which I wish to make is about Social Audit. In the entire country, communities should see to it that the money that is earmarked for the Panchayati Raj institutions is spent properly, and examine whether the money is spent on the purposes for which it is sent.

We have mentioned about the Panchayat Courts in our Act. Provisions have been made. There should be Panchayat Courts along with Panchayati Raj institutions so that those small disputes that arise between villagers are settled at the level of the village and the pressure on them is reduced, so that the people need not run to the courts, so that they need not spend a lot of money to get justice.

Our Panchayat Experience

I have not come here to teach you. I have come here to learn from you. I have travelled thousands of miles for this. But I would like to take this opportunity to share with you our experience about the State of the Panchayati Raj institutions in Jammu & Kashmir from where I come. Unfortunately the experience that we have is not a very good one. We have not done well in regard to Panchayati Raj. I will tell you the reasons for this.

In the inaugural session Mani Shankar Aiyar said that whenever there is a change of government at the State level the Panchayati Raj institutions are also made or marred. I agree with him and we have been victims of the same thing.

Fortunately ours is the first State in the entire country where a revolution was brought about, an agrarian revolution was brought about in which we gave lands to the tillers. We got this law passed in about 1950, that nobody can keep more than 182 hectare of land. The surplus land was distributed among the tillers without collecting any price whatsoever from them. All this was done under the leadership of our great leader Sheikh Abdullah whom we call the Lion of Kashmir. The surplus land was given to tillers if they had tillers, otherwise it was given to the landless. The important thing about this is that no price was collected from any one. This was such a big step. But the benefits would have been more if the scheme had been implemented through the process of democratic decentralistion. It would have made more progress and yielded better results if done through the Panchayati Raj institutions. Unfortunately Sheikh Sahib was arrested in 1953 and for about 20 to 22 years he was in jail. This adversely affected that process of democratic decentralization.

In 1975, Sheikh Sahib once again came to power. Immediately after coming to power he once again took steps towards democratic decentralization. The first thing he did was that he decentralized the planning and development process. He constituted District Development Boards. In these boards were members elected by the people, MLAs and MLCs and the members of Parliament. In those days, there used to be Block Development Boards, which are equal to your Taluk Panchayats, and then Chairmen of these Block Development Boards were the members of the District Development Boards. These District Development Boards used to prepare the plans for the respective districts. Whenever there was a review meeting of the Boards, Sheikh Sahib himself used to attend these meetings along with his cabinet colleagues. If any cabinet decision was necessary during the meetings of the boards, then the cabinet decision was taken then and there so that no time was lost.

After this Sheikh Sahib got elections to the Panchayati Raj institutions conducted, which had not been held for several years, nearly 10-15 years. Sheikh Sahib died in 1982. When fresh elections were held in 1983, once again the National Conference under the leadership of Dr. Farooq Abdullah formed the government. Unfortunately within 13 months that government was brought down. And the 13 persons who had defected from our party were all made ministers. And the first thing which the new government did was to dissolve the panchayats. They nominated some of their own persons in their places, and ran the institutions for three years.

Our New Panchayat Act

In 1981, we enacted a new Panchayati Act. In this Act the government was not given the power to dissolve panchayat institutions so that in future they did not dissolve any panchayats. We had taken this care when we enacted the 1981 Act. But unfortunately we could not conduct elections to these institutions. After a few months, President's Rule was imposed on the State. Hence, till 1986 elections could not be held either for the assembly or for the Parliament or for the Panchayati Raj institutions.

In 1986, fresh elections were held and once again our party came to power. Then we immediately started preparing to conduct elections to the Panchayati Raj institutions. We had to delimit the constituencies. A panchayat could not have more than 4,500 population if it is in the plains. Hence we had to carry out the delimitation exercise afresh. We also had to reconstitute the panchayats. Under very difficult circumstances we conducted elections to the Panchayati Raj institutions. The militants had given a call that whoever gets elected will be killed and that they will not rest till they are killed. Many panchas and sarpanchas were killed. Hence many became victims. In spite of this, the newly elected members and sarpanchas stayed their ground.

Our Struggle for Panchayats

In 2002 once again there was a change of government. Our party got the highest number of seats but not absolute majority. Hence there was a problem. Though we were told to form a coalition government, it could not be formed. A new coalition government was formed. Soon after the coalition government came to power, it decided to dissolve the panchayats for which we had conducted elections under very difficult circumstances. But since there was no provision in the Act which could be used to dissolve the panchayats, they introduced a bill in the assembly to empower the government to dissolve the elected panchayats whenever they wanted to. We stoutly opposed the bill. But we did not have majority. Hence, the bill was passed in the Assembly and as well as in the upper house.

Then the bill was sent to the Governor for his assent. We met the governor. I personally met him and told him that this kind of law is not found anywhere in the world under which an elected local panchayat can be dissolved by a government. Fortunately the Governor listened to us and he refused his assent to the bill. He also consulted the Union Panchayati Raj ministry. They also opined that such a law should not be made. We are thankful to the Union Panchayati Raj Ministry. However, though the designs of the government were not fulfilled, the Panchayati Raj institutions did not get any help or cooperation from the government. Hence, they could not do anything, they did not have the power. They were not given the money. They were harassed. This year the terms of these panchayats will end in the months of July and August. And according to our Act, one month before the term ends, elections will have to be conducted, i.e., in the month of June. But till today election notification has not been issued.

For the last eight months in Jammu and Kashmir there are no Panchayati Raj institutions. We are thankful to George Mathew that when he heard about it, he himself was ready to take the matter to the Court. He wanted to file a writ that there should be elections and people's representatives should be elected. Now after two years there are again assembly elections. I think we will have to wait till such a government comes to power which wants to have elections to the Panchayati Raj institutions. I am sure that you are also feeling sad listening to my story. I pray to God that the Panchayati Raj institutions here, particularly in Karnataka, should continue to serve the people, they should make progress, they should continue to solve the problems of the people. It is also my prayer that Karnataka should lead the entire country in the matter of Panchayati Raj institutions and in decentralization. I once again thank George Mathew and his friends for inviting me to this celebration of 20 years and for providing me with this opportunity of sharing my thoughts with you.

12

Panchayati Raj in Karnataka
Behind the Scene Actors

M.R. Sreenivasa Murthy

A.R. Rather has explained in detail the state of panchayats in Jammu & Kashmir. When we hear the woes of others our own sorrow is lightened. If we hear the story of the other 25 States we may feel still better, that we are far better off than many others. In my view, in spite of several problems facing the Panchayati Raj in Karnataka, our system is much better than those of many other States.

Not that there are no problems. One Savita Ramesh is enough. The whole day can be spent hearing about the problems. We have hundreds of problems. One may even feel that these animals called IAS officers are the cause of all these problems. These IAS officers have difficulty in telling the whole truth. They can only speak half-truths. That is why I was wondering how to tell the bitter truth when I speak. Luckily our senior leader and Home Minister Prakash, who spoke before me, lightened my burden by telling a major portion of that bitter truth.

I have been working gladly in this Panchayati Raj system since 1st April, 1987. I assumed office as the first Chief Secretary in the Mysore Zilla Parishad, which was very dear to Abdul Nazir Sab, on the 12th of February at a very inauspicious time. I worked happily in that Zilla Parishad for three years in the midst of several problems. Even now many friends coming from Mysore remember the days when we all worked together.

On this occasion I will speak about the IAS officers who have played and who are still playing their roles in this system. Many people said that the system in 1987 was very good but now it has deteriorated. You have heard about the efforts made by Ramakrishna Hegde and Abdul Nazir Sab to create this system in 1987. But behind them, behind the scenes, many IAS officers have slogged to draft the law, draft the rules, draft several circulars and government orders required for erecting the system. Not only IAS officers, but some non-IAS officers have also worked hard. On this occasion, I must mention the names of three such senior officers. Because please don't think that this system can work without the officers.

Officers Behind the Scene

T.R. Satish Chandran was the Chief Secretary at that time. He is living in our city even now. He retired as the Governor of Goa. As the Chief Secretary, he ably guided young officers like me on the working of the Panchayati Raj system. Not only that, he was also giving sound advice to Ramakrishna Hegde and Nazir Sab. They strove hard to see that the present system did not suffer like the earlier systems which were weak and inappropriate, but evolved as the true district government. Nobody mentions the name of T.R. Satish Chandran in this context . Because to work behind the curtains is the motto of our service. But when we are celebrating the two decades of the system it would be doing injustice to such persons if I do not mention their contributions.

The second one is P.R. Nayak. He was then the Development Commissioner and later he became the Additional Chief Secretary. He worked out the details of how much grant should be given to the Zilla Parishads, how much to the Mandal Panchayats, what should be the powers of the President, what should be the rights of the members, etc., by slogging over these matters for weeks together. Though the assent of the President was given to the Bill in

1985 the Panchayati Raj institutions could not become functional till 1st April, 1987. Officers were not idle these two years. They tried hard to make the preparations to see that the system worked efficiently once it was in place. Just a few months before the Zilla Parishads came into existence, T.R. Satish Chandran and P.R. Nayak, called officers like me to Mysore and told us that the Zilla Parishads were coming, and that we should play such and such role and explained how we should help these institutions. They trained us for weeks together. Decentralization of power does not take place by merely making a law. One has to work hard for it. That work was done by P.R. Nayak.

It is very important that I mention the third person. He was not an IAS officer. He was D.M. Nanjundappa. He and P.R. Nayak together called the Secretaries and Directors of each of the Departments and asked them how many officers their departments could spare for the Zilla Parishads, how many schemes they can hand over to the Zilla Parishads, why these personnel should not be transferred to the Zilla Parishads and Mandal Panchayats, etc. I have seen them doing this for months together. I was then the Director of a Department. They had asked me also as to how many schemes I was prepared to hand over to the Zilla Parishads, and to justify why I should keep them in my Department. I believe it was because these three senior officers and scores of other officers worked out the details of the Panchayati Raj system under the guidance of the government and implemented it with zeal, that the system earned the reputation of being the best in the country.

Officers are Equally Important

This system was in place for five years. In the Zilla Parishads in 19 districts it is the officers who worked as Chief Secretaries. Why do you say that when officers were there that system had worked well, today it is not working well? Then there were officers, and today also there are officers. Officers have to implement the policies of the existing government. Hence, I humbly would like to tell you that it would not be appropriate to say that the officers are responsible for the defects in the system.

Some people have said that they do not have power and have asked as to why the Government is interfering. Why does Taluk Panchayat interfere in the working of the Gram Panchayats or why does Zilla Panchayat interfere in the working of the Taluk Panchayats and why does the State Government interfere in the working of the Zilla Panchayats? Since I am outside any of these institutions, I do not find any difference. If all of you decide not to allow confusion in the system, there will be no confusion. M.P. Prakash has told you this in detail. What is the solution to this? Is there any defect in the law?

Why the Government issues Circulars

Our Constitution has given special powers to the Panchayats. The Constitution says that Panchayats can be given powers regarding 29 subjects. Which subject belongs to the Centre, which to the State, is clearly mentioned in the Constitution. Centre does not interfere in the subjects allotted to the States and the States do not interfere in the subjects allotted to the Centre. But this kind of division has not taken place between the States and the Panchayats. The subjects allotted to the States are also allotted to the Panchayat institutions. That is why the State Government makes laws, issues circulars, etc. We have to say that the powers have been given to the Panchayats. The Constitution says that any legislature can give any power to the Panchayats. There is a possibility that several conditions are imposed while making the law. Since the Central and State governments give grants one will have to listen to what they say. Why do you treat this as interference? The lack of clarity in the Constitution is the cause for this. To some extent this confusion is inevitable. If it is possible to bifurcate the powers of the State Government and the Panchayati Raj institutions then there may not be complaints that one is interfering with the other. As Prakash has said, any development in a system takes some time. We are in this kind of a situation. This system has still to evolve. It has to go forward. We have to bear this basic truth in our mind.

As an officer I would like to tell you a secret. In this situation, if all of you can be united and work together without any differences or conflict between the different tiers of the Panchayats then the work of rural development can proceed unhindered. Here everyone is talking about his rights, his powers. That is why one hears about dividing this thing among us, dividing that thing among us, give us this portion, you take that portion, etc. Please think about whether this is right. When the boundary between the powers of the State Government and the Panchayats is the same, or when their powers overlap, it is advisable that the State Government and the Panchayats work in tandem.

Many a time legislators have complained that they are not allowed to speak in the Panchayat meetings. Many have said that they have stopped attending the meetings of the Panchayats for this reason. Some have complained that they are told to speak in the legislative assemblies and not in the Panchayats. These are not good developments. Legally the legislators are the members of the Zilla Panchayats and Taluk Panchayats. When they participate in the meetings of these Panchayats, they should be given proper opportunities. Some legislators have said that when they give any advice or make any suggestion, they are ignored. When such advice or suggestions come, you should discuss them with the legislators and carry on development works with their cooperation. Doing this would be in the interests of the development of the Panchayati Raj system. If the conflict between one tier and the others continues, then the future of the Panchayati Raj cannot be good.

Can Panchayats become Local Governments?

It is said that the Panchayats should become local governments. But then, how difficult it is for an institution with Rs. 5 lakhs budget to be a government. When the urban areas are excluded and only rural areas are included, how difficult it is for these Zilla Panchayats to become governments ! Is the divide between the rural and urban advisable? In many countries, hundreds of villages surrounding a city are included in the Municipalities. In China there is a city called Tyanjin with a Municipal Corporation. When I was the Commissioner of Bangalore City Municipal Corporation, the Mayor of that City had visited Bangalore. He said that hundreds of villages surrounding his city had been included in the jurisdiction of the Tyanjin Municipal Corporation. It was a municipality only in name. It was carrying on all the duties of a government. But if we have three to four tiers of Panchayats, we cannot call them local governments.

If we want to establish local governments in our country in the real sense of the term, we should establish a strong government for one area and include in its jurisdiction all cities and towns and villages around it. If we have one Panchayat for municipal duties and one strong Panchayat in a district, they can grow well. Abdul Nazir Sab had talked about the four pillar State. But today we have seven to eight pillars. There is the Ward Sabha, then a Gram Sabha, then one Gram Panchayat and then a Taluk Panchayat and then a Zilla Panchayat. This is how it is structured. On top of these are the School Development Committees, Watershed Committees, Tank Water Users' Committees, an Akshara Dasoha Committee, etc., and if each one of them starts claiming to be a government then there will be too much confusion. We should make efforts to establish local governments. But if we have to establish them we will have to think differently. Dr. Mathew is the right person to organize a seminar on the difference between a local body and a local government. If we have to establish local governments, the question of "how a local government should function in the local context" has to be discussed. It is necessary that we have clear ideas about these things.

SECTION IV

Karnataka Panchayati Raj Elections

13

Old Memories

S.S. Meenakshisundaram

Twenty years ago, when Ramakrishna Hegde and Abdul Nazir Sab brought in the Panchayati Raj Act, I was working as Secretary in the department of Rural Development. That is why I am here today. When we started the Panchayati Raj system in Karnataka we did not get any response from the Central government. Because for them, this Panchayati Raj system was a new one. According to the Constitution this was a State subject and hence they said you better take care of it. Even when we wanted to conduct elections to the Panchayati Raj Institutions we did not get any cooperation from the Election Commission of India. We thought about what was to be done. We decided to conduct elections with the help of our district officers and establish the Zilla Parishads and Mandal Panchayats.

When the 73rd Amendment to the Constitution was passed, the same question arose once again. We thought, why should not the job of conducting elections to the Panchayati Raj Institutions be entrusted to the Election Commission. But the then Chief Election Commissioner said that they conduct elections only to the State legislatures and the Parliament and hence the elections to the Panchayati Raj Institutions should be conducted by the concerned States. Then the Prime Minister P.V. Narasimha Rao said that since the Election Commission was not willing to conduct elections to the Panchayati Raj Institutions we will appoint an election commissioner for each State. This is because those who conduct elections should not be part of the government.

The government is different and the Election Commission is different. It is only when both of them are independent of each other that it is possible to conduct free and fair elections. It is in this background that every State now has a State Election Commission. There have been already three election commissioners in our State. M.R. Hegde is the fourth State Election Commissioner. He will explain to you what problems are faced in conducting elections, what his experiences are, how he can help you and how you can help him in carrying out his work.

14

What You Should Know

M.R. Hegde

In Karnataka I am the Election Commissioner. You have been elected through the elections conducted by me. The Institute of Social Sciences has brought us face to face. I do not contest elections. I conduct elections. You contest elections.

It is self-evident that the panchayat elections should be conducted fairly and justly. Everyone desires this. But the job of the Election Commission does not end there. Meenakshisundaram has briefly told you about the 73rd amendment to the Constitution. It is not enough if elections are conducted. They should be conducted in time. Otherwise there was no need to amend the Constitution. In most of the States, elections are conducted 10 or 15 years after the terms of the Panchayats are over. In the background of that experience, this constitutional amendment came into force in 1993. The State Election Commission (SEC) came into existence. It was entrusted with the responsibility of conducting elections to all the local bodies. The State Election Commission has the same powers and authority as the Central Election Commission. The Constitution lays down what help and cooperation the State Government should extend to the SEC for conducting these elections.

Problems in Holding Elections

From 1993 till 2007, fourteen years have passed. Have the elections been conducted in time in these years? If not, what are the reasons? Is the Government responsible or is the State Election Commission responsible?

Three years have passed since I assumed office. Earlier, in the 11 previous years, perhaps once or twice elections have been held on time. Once the Gram Panchayat elections were postponed by about one year. After I assumed office, the elections were first held to the Gram Panchayats. It was held in time in February 2005. Even while conducting these elections, many writ petitions had been filed in our High Court. We had to get those petitions disposed of before holding elections. Thereafter the elections to the Zilla Panchayats and Taluk Panchayats had to be conducted before June 2005. By the time we set right the delimitation and reservation of the constituencies and were about to notify the elections, we received a stay order from the High Court. The High Court did not decide in our favour. Hence, we had to approach the Supreme Court, obtain stay of the order of the High Court and then conduct the elections in December 2005. Most of you have been elected in those elections.

Elections must be held in time. Because the Central and the State Governments give thousands of crores of rupees to the Panchayati Raj institutions. You have to decide as to how that money is to be utilized in rural areas for development. If members who have to take such decisions are not there in those institutions then what is the use of those institutions? That is why it is very essential that before the term of any Panchayat ends, elections must be held. Unfortunately, as far as I know, except in West Bengal, no other State Government has held elections in time.

Judiciary and Panchayat Elections

Recently, in October 2006, in Gujarat's Ahmedabad Corporation case, a full bench of the Supreme Court held that conducting elections in time is a constitutional obligation. In conducting those elections, the State Election Commissions have the same authority as that of the Central Election Commission. If the State Government does not extend any help then the State Election Commission can approach the High Court. If it does not get any relief in the High Court, it can approach the Supreme Court.

It is unfortunate that perhaps the High Courts do not consider the elections to the rural and urban local bodies as important. One or the other writ petition is filed, some stay order is granted, and the elections are postponed. Recently, as the Government delayed giving us the reservation list for the urban local body elections, we had to approach the High Court and obtain the reservation lists. The High Court gave us relief in just three weeks. This is the development after the decision of the Supreme Court. Perhaps now that the Supreme Court order has come, I hope the High Courts will hesitate to grant sudden stay orders to stop the elections.

To conduct elections to the Panchayats we have to make war-like preparations. There are 91,402 seats in the Gram Panchayats. In the elections held in 2005 there were 2,53,000 candidates. The seats in Zilla Panchayats and Taluk Panchayats were about 4,600 and the candidates numbered 16,000. We set up 1,92,000 polling stations. If you see this, you can understand the great extent to which we have to make preparations for conducting these elections.

If free and fair elections have to be held and in a peaceful manner, we mainly need the cooperation of the election staff. We give training through videos to this election staff, to the election officers, particularly during the Zilla Panchayat elections. This kind of training through video is perhaps the first of its kind in the whole country. We train all election officers on what is to be done from the date of filing of nominations till the counting of votes is over. We have also given them a handbook containing all the relevant acts and rules.

Candidates' Duty in Elections

All candidates have to declare their assets and liabilities. They have to declare the details of any criminal cases against them. All of you have done these things. But it has come to my knowledge that in many places, the affidavits have been defective. This has happened because even the election officers have not bothered to examine them. In some affidavits the candidates have not even signed. The candidates must be careful about such things. For the first time, we have used videos in the Zilla Panchayat elections. We had instructed the Deputy Commissioners that in very sensitive constituencies videos can be used. We have provided 5-6 video cameras to each of the Taluks. The Deputy Commissioners have reported that the move has been very effective.

During elections we have appointed persons to oversee the election expenses. We issued an order during the Zilla Panchayat and Taluk Panchayat elections and made it compulsory for the candidates to file election expenses. Even then, of the 16,817 candidates, more than 7-8 thousand candidates have not filed returns. Thereafter we have issued show cause notices to them. After the issue of show cause notices, the candidates get 20 days' time to file returns. Even then since many candidates did not file the returns, we have disqualified 1,440 Taluk Panchayat candidates and about 250 Zilla Panchayat candidates. We still have to decide about 30 per cent of the candidates. According to me this is a big number. I hope that the candidates will be more careful in future.

Officers and Elections

This time the Zilla Panchayat and Taluk Panchayat elections were held in a very competitive atmosphere. The main problem we faced came from the election staff. All the election staff remain under the disciplinary control of the State Election Commission for about a month only during the elections. Once the election results are declared we have no more control over them.

During the last Zilla Panchayat and Taluk Panchayat elections we have suspended 8 senior officers. For example, while filing your nominations you have to give the 'B' form from the party of which you are the candidate to the election officer. In one case, 8 candidates gave these forms to a Tahsildar who took them even though he was not the election officer. He did not hand over those forms in time to another Tahsildar sitting in the next room who was the election officer. As a result of this, we had to treat all those 8 candidates as independent candidates. This was a serious lapse. We do not know whether the Tahsildar did it on purpose or unknowingly. But we have suspended 8 such officers. When smaller lapses take place, we have recommended departmental enquiries against such officers.

Since day by day these elections are leading to serious conflicts, the election staff has to take care and see that serious lapses do not take place. A small lapse can lead to a big law and order problem. It has happened like that in many places. Whenever such lapses take place or whenever it comes to their knowledge that there may be small conflicts, the candidates and the general public should bring the same to our notice so that we can take necessary action in advance. In the last Zilla Panchayat elections, in Tumkur district, just two or three days before the elections, we got a Tahsildar transferred. When we take this kind of timely action it becomes possible to conduct free and fair elections without any conflict or riots.

Know the Election Law

The responsibility of the candidates is not over once they are elected. I have to decide on the questions of disqualification. I also have to decide if a seat becomes vacant. I wish to share with you one or two of my experiences. According to me, the members must have a minimum knowledge about the qualifications, disqualifications, the powers and responsibilities, etc. Your Panchayati Raj Act is in Kannada. You should study that Act. Otherwise, though you get elected as members, you will not be able to exercise your full powers.

I will give you one or two examples. You can be disqualified if you do not file returns of election expenses. About two weeks ago, a defeated woman candidate came to me and shouted that I had disqualified her and that I should take back the disqualification. I told her that once I pass an order disqualifying her, I cannot take it back and that she has to approach the High Court. Then I asked her about what her problem was. She said that she wanted to contest the Assembly elections and that the disqualification ordered by me would come in her way. I told her that she will have no problem because of two reasons. One was that one rule says that the disqualification will last for six years. The rule says that those who do not file their election expenses should be disqualified for six years. We cannot reduce the period. But there is another sub-rule which says that the disqualification will be effective for 3 years only though we disqualify a candidate for six years. Assembly elections are due in 2010. By that time her disqualification would have ceased to exist. Secondly, the disqualification in Panchayat elections is not taken into consideration for Assembly elections. Hearing this she was very happy and went away. You should know about such things.

Another issue concerns the disqualification for non-attendance in meetings. This complaint comes mostly from the faraway Gram Panchayats of Bidar district. Panchayat passes a resolution that a particular member was absent for three meetings. The Secretary writes about it. The Executive Officer of the Taluk Panchayat sends it to the State Election Commission. The Rule concerning this is very clear. If a member absents continuously for more than 3 meetings then he becomes disqualified and his seat becomes vacant. But in nearly 75-80 per cent of the cases that we receive, the Gram Panchayats send the proposal for disqualification as soon the member absents himself for *only 3 meetings*. Many Gram Panchayats send proposals for disqualifying 4-5 members at a time. We had sent a detailed circular in this regard. But unfortunately, neither the Gram Panchayat Secretary nor the Executive Officer of the Taluk Panchayat looks into it seriously. Disqualifying a member is a serious thing. The elected representative should not lose his position for some trivial reason or fault. But that is what is happening. That is why you should at least know about this one Act. This will help you in getting more actively involved in the development activities of the Panchayats.

A Word for Women

In our Panchayat elections more than 43 per cent women have got elected. You should know what your powers are. You should attend as many Panchayat meetings as you can. Rural areas have so many problems. There are problems of women, of children, of hospitals, of schools, of drinking water and so many others. If you involve yourselves in providing these facilities with the help of the grants given by the government you would be doing a great service to the society. Serving people is serving God. You should make the best use of this opportunity. I wish to tell women particularly, you have lot of patience, you have more commitment. You are more than 43 per cent of the total population. If you wish, you can change the very concept of rural development.

I end my speech with a couplet from poet Gundappa. It says, that the attraction of gold is very strong. But the attraction of male and female is stronger than that. But stronger still is the attraction of getting fame which actually eats into our soul. Don't bother too much about getting garlanded. If you do good work, people will respect you. You will become important persons. The post you occupy will become important. I wish to thank the Institute of Social Sciences for giving this opportunity to me and you for listening to me patiently. Thank you !

Question : You have disqualified Zilla Panchayat and Taluk Panchayat members for non-filing of return of election expenses. Why it is not done to the legislators? They also don't give correct information.

Answer : Legislators have to file their returns to the Central Election Commission. Only the Central Election Commission has the power to disqualify them. I do not have that power. But if the legislators do not file their returns, it does not mean that the Zilla Panchayat and Taluk Panchayat members also should not file their returns.

Q: According to the Constitution the elections have to be held on time. The High Courts and the Supreme Court also say the same thing. Then why does the Government not take the elections seriously. Why does the State Election Commission not take the Government to task for this?

Ans: State Election Commission has the responsibility of conducting the elections. Before the elections we have to do certain things. After every new Census, the number of constituencies increases. Hence, delimitation has to take place. Reservation has to be decided. We cannot hold elections on the basis of the reservations given in the previous election. Then there is lot of confusion about reservations, with sections saying that the Scheduled Castes should not be given reservation here, women should not be given reservation there, etc. You also expect the reservation pattern to change. Earlier fortunately the power to delimit the constituencies and decide on the reservations in Zilla Panchayats and Taluk Panchayats was with the State Election Commission. We did this in the 2005 elections. We were about to announce that the election process should be completed before June. At that time we received a stay order from the High Court. After receiving the stay order I could not do anything. Had I done something, it would have amounted to contempt of court. Afterwards we approached the Supreme Court and obtained a stay and conducted the elections.

Q: You prepare the voters' lists for the rural areas every year. But when new lists are prepared nearly 10 per cent of names are missing from the list. I do not know whether this is done purposely or by mistake. One may have an Identity

Card but one's name will not be there in the list. Once a person's name is entered in the list, he should have the right to vote till his death. State Election Commission should do something about this.

Ans: We have to conduct Panchayat elections on the basis of the electoral lists prepared for the assembly elections. If there are defects in the electoral rolls of the assembly then the defects continue in the Panchayat elections also. We cannot change them. Central Election Commission has to change them. But then, till the last date of filing nominations names can be added to or deleted from the lists. But people are not vigilant about it. How many people go and see the voters' lists? Even in cities nobody does it. Only on the day of the election we go and see the lists. At that time nothing can be done.

Q: In Gram Panchayats there are multi-member constituencies. Persons from general category as well as from the Scheduled Caste category can contest. In case there are two Scheduled Caste category candidates, the one who gets less votes between the two, but gets more votes than the candidate in the general category, such a Schedule Caste candidate is considered to have been elected from the general category seat. Why is it so?

Ans: This happens because of Rule 72. This will continue to happen till the rule is changed or till we have only single member constituencies.

Q: If a Gram Panchayat member dies, in how many days after that elections do have to be held?

Ans: We get information about the death of a Gram Panchayat member from the Deputy Commissioner. After that we conduct elections within 3 or 4 months.

Q: Can a person who is working as a government lawyer contest elections to the Zilla Panchayat and after getting elected can he continue to work as the government lawyer?

Ans: Government lawyers cannot contest any elections. When the nomination papers are scrutinised, if any other person contesting the election points this out, then his papers can be rejected. Even now he is disqualified but now an enquiry will have to be held.

Q: I have been elected twice. A person was elected from the general seat and became the President. Thereafter the Presidentship was reserved for persons belonging to the backward classes. Now the same President, has again become the President by producing a certificate that he belongs to the backward class. Is this right?

Ans: The Supreme Court had once given a judgement that if the Presidentship is reserved for a particular category, only persons who get elected from seats reserved for that category can contest the elections to the Presidentship. But within six months the Supreme Court changed that decision. In the new decision the Supreme Court said that if a person getting elected from a general category belongs to the category for which the Presidentship is reserved, he can also contest the election to the Presidentship. This is what has happened in your Panchayat. He can contest the election by producing the certificate that he belongs to the category for which the Presidentship is reserved.

Q: Some influential persons in the village and sometimes even the Gram Panchayat Secretary do not allow women to file nominations from the general seat. They say you file nomination for the seat reserved for women. Is it right to say this?

Ans: It is wrong to do that.

Q: There is another serious problem. Whenever the Presidentship of a Panchayat is reserved for a particular category, there will be a conspiracy to see that the candidates belonging to that category are not available to contest the election. For example, if the Presidentship is reserved for repair works, etc. They said that money should not be spent for supply of water also. When our Federation wrote to the State Election Commission about this, we received a reply within three days that since the elections to the Gram Panchayats are not held on party basis, these restrictions do not apply but then nothing should be done to promote a particular candidate, etc. This has helped in the entire State. I thank the State Election Commission for this.

2. When the State Election Commission decides on the reservation, if a seat is reserved for the backward classes, it is reserved for women belonging to the backward classes. Men do not get a chance to contest in such seats. But in seats reserved for women belonging to the backward classes, only women belonging to that class can contest. This is not fair.
3. Today educated persons also become Presidents and uneducated persons also become Presidents. But whatever letter comes to the Panchayat it comes to the Secretary. Hence, both the educated and the uneducated Presidents have to ask the Secretary about the contents of the letter. Please ensure that in future the letters are sent to both the Secretary and the President.
4. Every 3 months, the Presidents, Vice-Presidents and the Secretaries of the Gram Panchayats at the Taluk level used to have meetings with the Executive officer and the Chief Executive Officer of the Taluk Panchayat and Zilla Panchayat respectively. But the decisions taken in the meetings are never implemented. I request the State Election Commission and the Rural Development and Panchayati Raj Department to set this right.
5. There is not even a single family belonging to the Scheduled Tribes in our village. However, one seat is reserved for the women belonging to the STs.

women, they conspire to see that no woman is available to become the President and then the Vice President continues to run the Panchayat for many years. This is a universal truth. The State Election Commission should take notice of this. Can something be done to avoid this? Is it possible to conduct fresh elections whenever a candidate belonging to a particular category is not available? Can the State Election Commission do anything to see that the advantages of reservation which have been given to ensure social justice are made available to the concerned categories? In my Taluk, till today in one Panchayat, the Vice President is carrying on the administration. By this we are depriving a class of persons permanently. You should take this seriously.

Ans: I do not have the power to reserve Presidentships and Vice Presidentships. Even then I would like to give my views. First of all, basically in my view, the term of office of the President and the Vice President should be a complete 5 years. Because any term of less than 5 years will not be sufficient for a person to gain good experience of the office. But here the term of office of Presidents is in some places 20 months. In some places they are not allowed to complete 20 months also. After 10 months one person is made to resign or is removed by no-confidence motion and another is elected in his place. That means, in a period of one and a half to two years, there will be 5 Presidents and 5 Vice Presidents. In my opinion this is not good for the health of the Panchayati Raj system. The Government has the power to reserve seats. If a person of a particular category is purposely not made available then you should write to the Government. We have no role in electing the Presidents and the Vice Presidents.

Views from the Floor

1. When the elections to the Gram Panchayats were held last time, the local officers decided to stop all works by the Gram Panchayats. They did not allow any meetings to be held, or to carry out day-to-day work,

Hence, we had to bring a woman belonging to the STs from a neighbouring village and get her elected. So when deciding on the reservation please see that it is done on the basis of the population of the different categories in the village.

SECTION V
Karnataka Innovative Practices

15

A Village Panchayat's Wall Street Journal

Na. Li. Krishna

I have been asked to speak on the innovative practices that are growing in the Panchayats. I wish to share some of my experience in this regard. The root of today's panchayats is in the Gram Sabhas. But we are hearing from everywhere that these Gram Sabhas are very colourless and are taking place in an atmosphere of conflict. What is the reason for this? Ward Sabhas and Gram Sabhas are also innovative practices. Ashokanand was saying that even democracy is a new system for us. We have been ruled by Rajas and Maharajas for the past 300-400 years. After that the British who came to India for carrying on trade ruled us. It is only in the last 50 years that we are ruling ourselves in a democratic system. Hence, even democracy is a new practice.

Today Ward Sabha and Gram Sabha are new concepts for people. The Ward Sabha and Gram Sabha will be successful if we can convince the people about their importance, that it is important that they should participate in it, to know what is their responsibility in them, and more than all this, that if the Ward Sabha and Gram Sabha can be conducted successfully with participation of the people, it would be very effective in bringing about rural development. If the Panchayat representatives and the Government can create that kind of an atmosphere, these Sabhas can be successful. But the misfortune is that we are hearing that the Ward Sabhas and Gram Sabhas are failing.

I have heard, however, that they are being successfully conducted in many parts of the State. I have seen how these meetings are conducted with total transparency. It is said that in connection with the selection of beneficiaries of housing schemes, there is corruption and nepotism. But most of the Panchayats in the State are selecting the beneficiaries of the housing schemes transparently after discussion in the Ward Sabhas and Gram Sabhas. There are Panchayats which have video graphed these meetings. They have sent a copy of the CD of these videographs along with the list of the beneficiaries to the government and have retained a copy of the CD for their own records. Such Panchayats should be taken as models whose example should be followed.

To give an example, today in the Gram Panchayat of which Ravikumar is the President, since morning the complaints against the Secretary are flowing like a river in spate. In contrast, Madhusudan, who, though working in two Gram Panchayats of Annur and Nagarakere, has earned the glory of putting both these Panchayats at the top position in the State. If we go on discussing about these kinds of possibilities, I think the Panchayati Raj system will get strengthened.

About conducting general meetings, the Panchayati Raj Act mentions two points. Free atmosphere and transparency should be created in conducting these meetings. The President has the freedom to keep the general public outside in order to conduct the meeting properly. Since a new generation has now entered these Panchayat institutions, the general meetings these days are being conducted in a very free atmosphere. In most of the Panchayats, the windows are kept open to allow the general public to participate in the proceedings. When such a free atmosphere is created, people develop respect for their representatives. They realize that the representatives elected by them are working with responsibility and within the framework of the law.

Jamabandi is a system of social audit. That also has to be conducted in the presence of the general public. The works undertaken by the Panchayats, other dealings, expenditure on salary, conveyance and all accounts should be presented to the people and should be subjected to analysis. How much money has been spent, whether street lights have been put up, whether the motor has been repaired, whether the hand pump has been repaired? Keeping all these details in front of the people is *Jamabandi*. Earlier there was a tradition of issuing a small handbill stating as to on what date the *Jamabandi* will take place, which are the officers who will participate in it, and inviting the President and members of the Panchayat and the general public of the village to participate in it. The new practice is to publicize the event in a big way, informing the people that they should participate in the *Jamabandi*, they should find out the truth, they should ask questions. They are told about what information they can get, and if *Jamabandi* programme can be systematically and successfully carried out then it should be possible to prevent a Gram Panchayat from going astray.

•

Corruption in Panchayats

Representatives here are saying in this forum, without any hesitation, without any embarrassment, that with the decentralization of power decentralization of corruption and nepotism have also taken place. But there are Panchayats in our State which are different. There are Panchayats which have been declared to be corruption-free. It is necessary to seriously discuss about such panchayats in this type of meeting. We should develop a tradition of identifying such Panchayats and discussing them in the legislative assembly. If that happens, then the Panchayats will get moral support, and others will also start thinking of creating such corruption-free and fearless Panchayats. I wish to humbly bring to your notice that ours is one of the few Panchayats which have been declared to be corruption-free in our State.

People lack knowledge, they lack information. They do not have the details of the various schemes. What is the procedure for getting the *khata* of a house in a village? How to get *khata* transferred to another name? How to get a No

Objection Certificate. How to get a certificate? What is the fee prescribed for it? How is the water tax levied? How is the house tax levied? With whose money is the drainage being maintained? It is the responsibility of our Panchayat representatives to explain all these things to our villagers. Earlier these kinds of things were done with the help of the village headman, or a literate person. But today when a new generation of representatives have entered the Panchayat institutions, they are trying to publish a paper to maintain their transparency. The Nagarakere and Annur Gram Panchayats of Maddur Taluk have started a new practice of publishing a wall newspaper once every month.

Effectiveness of Sub-Committees

If we have to strengthen the decentralization of power, then power will have to flow to the last of the citizens of this State. Now, in Panchayats, sub-committees have been formed. In these sub-committees, along with the members of the Panchayats, there are ordinary villagers who have been made members. Water Cleanliness Committee, Production Committee, Facilities Committee, etc., have been formed. Earlier the fishing rights of a pond in Nagarakere Gram Panchayat were auctioned for Rs. 900 per year. Now the ponds have been entrusted to the Gram Panchayats. Local people have learnt how much the production is, what is the profit, etc., and as a result of this, last month, we auctioned publicly the fishing rights for Rs. 30,000 for three years. Because Gram Panchayats were empowered, today we could get Rs. 10,000 per year. This way these Production Committees are very helpful in mobilizing resources.

A person living in the village understands better as to where the water problem is, where a bore well has to be sunk, etc., than the legislator. We have constituted a Food Vigilance Committee for every ration shop in the village under the guidance of the Social Justice Committee. Through these committees the people are being educated and made aware about the quantity of food grains that have been allotted to a ration shop, in what quantities the same has to be distributed to the people and at what price, and that people should insist on cash bills, etc. The Committee called a meeting of all the ration shop owners in the Gram Panchayat area and told them that whatever wrong things they were doing all these days should be stopped, and that they should cooperate with the people. The Committee has been very successful in its work.

Our Journal : *Grama Sarakara*

We are bringing out a monthly wall journal called *Grama Sarakara* through our Panchayat. The purpose of the journal is to inform the people about the programmes of the Panchayat. The journal is pasted on the walls in places where more people gather, like the bus stand, hotels, milk dairy, etc. In the first issue we published the prices of foodgrains and other items which were available in the ration shops. Our Panchayat has prepared a budget for Rs. 40 lakh in March. Many people do not know what is in the budget. We have mentioned in this journal as to what amount is being spent on which programme, etc. I conclude with a wish that the power may flow to the lowest levels through such innovative practices.

16

Village Level Planning

K. Ravikumar

The experiments being conducted by these three neighbouring Gram Panchayats, i.e., Nagarakere, Kyataghatta and Annur, are influencing one another. Much discussion has taken place about preparation of plans with the participation of the people, the possibilities and the opportunities that it has, etc. Today we have to prepare plans with the participation of the people. I had a very sad feeling that though the Government has been issuing circulars in this regard since 2001, it has not been possible for the local bodies to prepare development plans.

I decided to do something about it. So I started discussing it in the Ward Sabhas and Gram Sabhas. We faced many problems while preparing this plan. We did not have enough data. I discussed with a senior friend, Janardhan of Udipi, as to how to collect this data and prepare a model. When Raghunandan was Secretary in the Rural Development and Panchayati Raj Department of Government of Karnataka he had issued an order that there should be a revision of Panchayat properties. Still nothing had been done about it.

We thought that if we can prepare the plan also along with the revision of the properties it would be very effective. We then completely revised all the Panchayat properties. We had to face a lot of opposition at the time of revision. *Why do you want all this? You are revising the valuation of the properties in the guise of collecting taxes,* said some people very seriously. We tried to convince the people that the Gram

Panchayats have to mobilize their own resources today. We have to take care of the drinking water, we have to take care of the street lighting. All these are becoming very difficult. If we want to function as local governments we will have to become self-sufficient, etc.

With the help of the Abdul Nazir Sab Institute of Rural Development in Mysore, we discussed how to prepare a plan, what should be given priority, etc. Many people had many demands when we were preparing the plan. We said that all demands cannot be fulfilled in one year and we have only so many resources, and only so many opportunities. We finally prepared the plan. We could not fulfil all the aspirations of our villagers in the plan. We also fell behind in implementing it. But within the resources available to us, we prepared a plan that gave priority for creating assets, for training, for the handicapped, for the Scheduled Castes and Scheduled Tribes, for cottage industries, etc. We faced many difficulties in preparing and implementing this plan.

The Non-Co-operating Officers

When Malati Das and V.P. Baligar were the secretaries of the Rural Development and Panchayati Raj department, they had issued orders that the *Jamabandi* officers should participate in the preparation of the plans. But how many officers are participating in it? In our Taluk when we said that we have initiated this kind of a plan, even our Executive Officer did not cooperate. He did not encourage us. He did not congratulate or appreciate us for being the first to have initiated this process in the entire district. He did not bother to ask what help we wanted. This attitude has really pained us. Only some officers whom we knew personally helped us.

Today it is necessary that there should be coordination between the departmental schemes and the Panchayats. If that happens, the schemes become stronger. They say that Kerala is the model for the entire nation. The reasons for that are the powers given to the Panchayats, the way the people think and the commitment and concern of the officers.

This plan of our Gram Panchayat should become part of the entire district's development plan. But how many District Planning Committees are functional today? The government is issuing circulars since 2001 that the District Planning Committees should become active. But still they are not active. If the District Planning Committee is not active then only the lower level development planning is of no use. Even many Gram Panchayats are not in a position to prepare their own plans today. Because our Secretaries are not capable. We have to build the capacity of these secretaries and the representatives of the people also. It is only then that the schemes and programmes can be implemented effectively.

The Secretaries have to be trained regularly to improve their capabilities and inculcate farsightedness, a change of mindset in them. We talk very lightly about the Secretaries that work at the lowest levels. We look down upon them. None of us are capable of talking to the Executive Officers of the Taluk Panchayats and the Chief Executive Officers of the Zilla Panchayats. But we indulge in complaining and punishing harshly the Secretaries of the Gram Panchayats.

Lastly, Minister Udasi said yesterday that the Presidents should be directly elected. But if that happens I wish to impress upon you that we will have to contend with tyranny in the villages once again. Thank you !

17

Removing Encroachments

H.B. Madhusudhan

I have the singular misfortune of working at the lowest levels of rural areas and carrying on my head the highest number of complaints. I was appointed as the Gram Panchayat Secretary on compassionate grounds in 1998. I assumed charge on 8th November, 2005 as the Secretary of the Annur Gram Panchayat which had earned a very good reputation at the State level. There were 18 members in the Panchayat who had been elected unanimously. They had received a two-day training through satellite. Hence, they insisted on mobilizing the resources. They enquired from me as to what were the policies and guidelines of the State Government on mobilization of resources. They asked me to cooperate with them for mobilizing the resources.

From then on, just within three months, we undertook the task of levying tax on a sugar factory which had been established within the jurisdiction of our Gram Panchayat. We served the first notice on them on 30th of November. The management of the factory gave a funny answer to that notice. The correspondence between the factory and the Gram Panchayat continued. A sugar factory which was situated on a land measuring 46 acres 16 *gunthas* was paying only Rs. 35,000 per year to the Gram Panchayat. This cheating had continued for the past 30 years. A determined struggle was necessary to set this injustice right. All the members of the Gram Panchayat got united. With a single mindedness they used my services also and undertook the task of revising the tax. We held several meetings. We visited several big factories and studied them.

Thereafter we issued a notice demanding Rs. 9,99,225. The factory management said that this was about a hundred times more than what they were paying and that we should reduce the demand to about 3 to 4 lakh.

We had to discuss this in the Gram Sabha. The moral support of the Gram Sabha was with us. They said unless you levy a reasonable tax on the sugar factory you cannot collect a single paisa as tax from the villagers. They said that if the Panchayat was finding it difficult, we should tell them and that they would all stand behind us solidly. They said that they cannot tolerate the cheating by the factory any more and that taking support of the entire villagers the Gram Panchayat should collect the tax from the factory.

As a result of this exercise we agreed to reduce the tax to Rs. 7.50 lakh per year and collected the first cheque from the factory on 28th March. How was this possible? When the members of the Gram Panchayat take a decision with one mind, the general public extends their moral support to them. Under such circumstances a situation is created in which any unfair system in place will have to bend. This is the best example.

Revision of Taxes

The Secretary to the department of Rural Development and Panchayati Raj, Raghunandan, had sent a circular in May 2003 that there should be a revision of all the properties of the panchayats. In the last para of the circular there was a sentence. It said that the Gram Panchayats can tax even the transformers in the sub-stations of the Karnataka Power Transmission Corporation Limited, built within the limits of the Gram Panchayat.

On the basis of the said circular, we issued a notice to the Bangalore Electricity Supply Company which had built a transformer on the land belonging to the Gram Panchayat.

Once again there was a long correspondence between the Gram Panchayat and BESCOM. They had not paid any tax for the past 9 years. After prolonged discussions an agreement was reached between us. We submitted a demand of Rs. 1,87,320 and decided on an annual tax of Rs. 33,000. Peoples' participation becomes possible only if the Gram Panchayats try to do something good. It is only then that the Gram Panchayat can proceed on the path of development.

Removing Encroachments

One President did all this and resigned. Another President was elected. Between them there was a healthy competition. The new President said that if there was revision of property tax under the previous President, he would concentrate on the environmental and development issues during his presidency. Just the previous month we had received a circular from the government. It said that the Gram Panchayats should take action to remove encroachments on the Gram Panchayat properties. We discussed this in the Gram Sabhas and distributed handbills about it to every house. We began removing encroachments and when we did it for one or two houses, the others themselves started removing their encroachments. We have video graphed our actions. This became possible because of the united efforts of the Gram Panchayat and the participation of the people.

There was some opposition also. In one place an elderly woman threatened the President saying *you are my elder brother's son. Because we gave you an opportunity, you have become the President. Now you have come to demolish my compound wall. If you demolish my compound wall I will commit suicide by hanging myself.* But the President had the support of all the members of the Gram Panchayat. Whatever decision the President took all the members would support him. The President told that woman, *please do not hang yourself. I will resign from the Presidentship. Then some one else will become the president. He will also come to demolish your compound wall. He will demolish it. Will you then hang yourself.*

No body can stop the work of removing the encroachments. In this connection I will not hang on to any relationship. Encroachment must be removed now. Saying thus he started the work of removing the encroachment.

At this time, some women's groups in the village got ready to ban liquor within the jurisdiction of the Gram Panchayat. As a result of their efforts, soon we took 3,000 villagers to the office of the Deputy Commissioner and submitted a memorandum. Within a week, the Deputy Commissioner sent the Superintendent of Excise to our village and got all the licenses of the liquor vendors in the village cancelled. Our Gram Panchayat became a liquor-free Gram Panchayat.

On 29th of last month, when a factory started constructing one of its units without the permission of the Gram Panchayat we again called a Gram Sabha which took a very important decision and stood in support of us. About 1,000 villagers agitated that the factory should stop construction of the unit as it had not taken the permission of the Gram Panchayat and succeeded in stopping the construction. We also did a good job with the ration system which became a model.

Gram Panchayats also have the responsibility of giving information to the people. In fulfilment of this responsibility, the two Gram Panchayats of which I was the Secretary, started publishing the periodical *Gram Sarakara* which has been mentioned by Na. Li. Krishna. Thus we are reaching information to every house in the villages of our two Gram Panchayats. When we keep the villagers informed like this, they lean towards the Gram Panchayats, they respect Gram Panchayats. In the midst of all this, the Annur Gram Panchayat could also host a State level convention of the Grama Swarajya Vedike in our village. I would like to conclude by emphasizing that all this was possible because of the unity of the members of the Gram Panchayat and the participation and cooperation of the people of the villages. Thank you !

18

We Banned Liquor

Kamala

When I became the President of my Gram Panchayat, the first reaction of the people was will this small girl sitting in the chair be able to run the Gram Panchayat? After I heard this I took a very bold decision and due to that decision taken on that day I am here today on the stage. My prime desire as the woman President of my Gram Panchayat was to give priority to women.

Since ours is a very backward area Gram Panchayat, the people there were very much addicted to drinking. They would waste Rs. 50 on drinking and the remaining Rs. 10 would go for running the household which was not at all sufficient. When I was wondering how to stop this drinking habit, how to bring awareness among women about this, many women's organizations also joined chorus with me. What I could not achieve as a villager I set about to achieve as the President of the Gram Panchayat. I knew that we had to struggle quite a lot to ban liquor from our villages. However, much we begged people, liquor would land in our village from somewhere.

The liquor vendors would say that they would bring liquor from somewhere and that we had no business asking them about it. When I asked them if they had taken licenses from the Gram Panchayat they said that since they had good income from vending liquor they would give me Rs. 3,000 every month and that I should keep quiet. I told them that I was not interested in their bribe and that no liquor should be brought within the Gram Panchayat's limits. I told them that the liquor was destroying the lives of women in the villages. Their families were being destroyed. Whatever threats I held out against them, they would still bring liquor in the dead of the night and keep it in the shops. Once we even tried to set fire to their shops. Even that did not deter them.

The Vigil at Night

Once we womenfolk decided to confront them in the dead of night itself. The menfolk in the village had warned women that they should not go out of the house in the night. Even then hundreds of women joined hands with me and we set out at 11 o'clock at night. We confronted the vendors bringing liquor and stopped them on the road. We told them that if they step into our village any more we would burn their shops and the liquor. As a result of this bold step we succeeded in stopping the vending of liquor in our villages and we could ban liquor. In the same way, about 150 women's organizations in the Taluk joined hands and launched a struggle against liquor. The trouble we underwent those days has brought us results and a sense of satisfaction to us.

Ashraya scheme had been given to the Gram Panchayats. Today we have seen to it that all huts in all the 22 villages of our Gram Panchayats have been replaced by houses. The scheme has reached the deserving people. Many poor people told me that earlier they would petition for houses and nobody bothered. But now the beneficiaries were being directly selected in open Gram Sabhas. Once without our knowledge, even the Chief Planning Officer from the Zilla Panchayat came and sat in one of our Gram Sabhas and saw as to how we were conducting the Gram Sabhas and selecting the beneficiaries.

Under the Nanjundappa Committee Report, Kunigal Taluk has been declared a backward taluk. Hence, we prepared an action plan for five years after discussing the same in Ward Sabhas and Gram Sabhas with full participation of the people and in accordance with their conveniences and requirements. Nowadays so many men and women attend our Ward Sabhas and Gram Sabhas. Earlier people would come to the Gram Sabha, pose for the photograph and go away. It was difficult to get 20-25 people to attend the Gram Sabha. Now the Gram Sabha which starts at 11 A.M. does not show the signs of ending even after 3 P.M. There is so much of participation by the people.

When we inform people how much of grant we are receiving and for what we are giving priority, people start trusting us more. Then people said, *this girl is working so well. We should give her more cooperation.* In the same way, the wall periodical *Grama Sarakara* being published by our friends has also been of great help to us. Instead of criticizing women as to what they can or cannot do, if people extend their cooperation to them women can show what they can achieve.

In some neighbouring Gram Panchayats women were not speaking at all. After interacting with us, now they are talking more. I would like to conclude by saying that when information is given, when power is given, when cooperation is extended, women can also achieve anything.

19

Power of Information

Krishna M. Ittangi

Earlier our Gram Panchayat meetings were taking place once in six months or once in eight months. But now most of the elected members of the Panchayats are youngsters. They are contesting the Panchayat elections and participating in the Panchayati Raj system with belief in the system and with a view to do some service to the villagers and not with any intention of grabbing power. Earlier the Patels and Gowdas were ruling. Power to them was a matter of prestige. After Ramakrishna Hegde became the Chief Minister, he gave a new turn to this Panchayati Raj system. He gave reservation to women, to the backward classes, to the deprived classes in the system. He decentralized democracy so that all people could get elected, participate and exercise power in the system. Today our elected representatives of the Panchayats are trying to fulfil his dream.

I come from a very backward district of Koppal in Hyderabad Karnataka area. Earlier Panchayat meetings were not taking place at all. After we got elected, we convinced all the members and now the meetings are taking place every month without fail. Some friends here told us that they are trying to inform the people about the Panchayat's activities through a wall paper. But we are following a different method. Along with the meeting notice, we are sending the proceedings of the earlier meetings and the Income and Expenditure Statement of the Gram Panchayat. Our members are sharing this information with their neighbours. This has increased the transparency. We are also giving information about how much money has been spent on which of the schemes, etc. Thus we are trying to carry on the administration of our Gram Panchayat transparently.

Earlier the legislators were distributing houses to their followers and friends. But in the present system, we are distributing the houses through the Gram Sabhas. Hence we are confident that the houses are reaching the most deserving people. In a Gram Sabha it becomes evident as to whether a beneficiary is a rich man or is a relative of the President of the Gram Panchayat. We are also videographing the proceedings of these Gram Sabhas. When our Minister Udasi visited Koppal district, he came to our village and has seen the videos.

Even the Principal Secretary M.R. Shreenivasa Murthy had come to our village and has seen the arrangements made by us. He has patted our backs and encouraged us. But now the legislators are pressurizing the government to hand over the power of selecting the beneficiaries to a committee headed by them. If the selection committees are constituted with legislators at the head, they will hand over the contract of constructing the houses to whomsoever they like and get a commission from them. Now the commission has stopped. Hence, their struggle now is about restoring it. We have been given the power to select the beneficiaries only about a year ago. We are doing now what the legislators could not do in the last 15 years. We are now transparently checking at every stage of the construction and only then releasing the cheques. Legislators are unable to tolerate this. Though we are working so transparently and honestly, instead of encouraging us, it is unfortunate that the legislators are demanding taking over these powers themselves. As legislators they have a lot of things to do. Let them do those things and leave the Ashraya committees to us.

Another issue is that there is a shortage of staff in Gram Panchayats. You are giving one Secretary for two to three Gram Panchayats. This should be avoided. We welcome transfer of more powers to us. But along with the powers, please give us staff also. I understand that in the next two years, 80 per cent of the posts of secretaries will fall vacant. When will the government appoint them? The government should take more interest in this and fill the vacancies as early as possible. Please give us the powers, please give us the staff and then see whether we will work or not. Instead of that, you are trying to kill the baby before it grows up. I would like to say that this is very wrong. Thank you !

20

Our Give and Take Movement

S.R. Hiremath

I have been working with several organizations for the past 25 years in the field of rural development and environment. We have built an organization in this State called *Grama Ganarajya Vedike*. The inspiration for the organization was the debate in our Constituent Assembly about the Panchayati Raj system that extended for ten full days. Another inspiration was Article 40 of our Constitution. In addition to these, the work of many important personalities and their experiences, particularly the path breaking enactment brought by Abdul Nazir Sab and his efforts to put it in practice. As a result of all these inspirations, the 73rd amendment to the Constitution was passed unanimously in the Lok Sabha and Rajya Sabha in December 1992.

Though 10-15 years have elapsed since, the system has not been put in place properly. As the Central and State governments are self-governing bodies, the Panchayati Raj institutions also should be self-governing bodies. But there has been no significant decentralization of power till now. There has been no economic decentralization. There has been no devolution of staff. If these three do not happen, local bodies cannot function as units of self-government.

Some prominent citizens like former Chief Justice of Karnataka High Court, D.M. Chandrasekhar, C. Narayanaswamy, L.C. Jain, B.K. Chandrasekhar, etc., submitted a report to the government. Its main purpose was to strengthen the Ward Sabhas and Gram Sabhas. Siddharaj

Dhadda had appended a small separate note to Asoka Mehta Committee's report and had said that the base of the Panchayati Raj system was the Gram Sabha. He had said that in Gram Sabha there was scope for the general public to participate in governance, i.e., the general public will have an opportunity to practice direct democracy.

In this background we had tried to get the Panchayati Raj Act amended. Our efforts were successful and with the help of the ministers and senior officers in the government the amendments were finally accepted in 2003. As a result of these amendments, today the decisions taken in the Gram Sabhas are considered final decisions.

Secondly, with the efforts of officers like Chiranjeevi Singh, V.P. Baligar, and particularly the efforts in the Assembly of members like D.R. Patil and Dr. Sharanaprakash Patil, etc., the Panchayati Raj system has an opportunity to spend Rs. 1,900 crore. Earlier it was difficult to get more money. Now *Jamabandi* is being organized to see that the money is used properly. Mahatma Gandhi had said in 1931 that the biggest obstacle in bringing *grama swaraj* was the officers who were not willing to part with their powers. After a pause of few moments he said, that power belonged to us, it is our birth right and that we should become capable of getting it. As a result of this, the *Give and Take* movement started. Every year, people from the four corners of Karnataka come to Bangalore, to Davanagere, to Ranebennur, to Gokak, to Nagnur and try to enhance their capabilities, to get power from the State government. This is very important. Because only when people struggle and get something, do they realize its importance. Then that power is likely to be used properly. Yesterday, even the Principal Secretary of the Rural Development and Panchayati Raj Department said the same thing.

The powers between the State government and the Panchayati Raj institutions have not been distributed in our Constitution as has been done in the case of Central and

State governments. We have to think about how to get this done. The non-cooperation and civil disobedience movements of Mahatma Gandhi had impacted the then British government considerably. We must retain that tradition. Panchayati Raj should evolve into a people's movement.

As people participated in our freedom struggle, people must participate in the Panchayati Raj movement also and get their powers and use them properly. I conclude by saying that we should together strive to achieve this goal.

SECTION VI
Concluding Session

21

International Centre for Local Governance and Nazir Sab Chair

George Mathew

Bangalore has become one of the most important cities in the country. Bangalore has a moderate climate, beautiful gardens, wonderful people and, above all, it is the seat of the government which introduced the most radical local government system in the country. Since Ramakrishna Hegde and Abdul Nazir Sab took a pioneering step in bringing the rural population to the centre stage, Karnataka State has become a pilgrim centre of advocates and practitioners of decentralization and local government. From many countries, they continue to come to Bangalore, Mysore and other parts of the State.

Therefore, my request to the Government of Karnataka is to help us establish an International Centre for Local Governance in Bangalore. This will be a centre of excellence on local governance where :

- national and international local governance narratives will be analysed;
- exchange of experience from all over the world will take place;
- discourses and debates on ideas of local communities, local governments, grassroots democracy, fiscal decentralization, and inclusion of excluded communities as well as women's participation will be conducted to generate a

knowledge base for effective local government at the local, regional, national as well as international levels.

This Centre in Bangalore will attract international attention at a time when decentralization and local governance have come to the fore to meet the Millennium Development Goals, and as the best instrumentality for good governance. The people of Karnataka and the local government system in this State will immensely benefit from such a Centre.

When we are remembering Abdul Nazir Sab, one of the great sons of Karnataka, may I request the Government of Karnataka to establish a chair in his name. The Institute of Social Sciences, New Delhi, has a beautiful hall dedicated to Nazir Sab's memory. It is time that we attract the best of minds on decentralization and local governance to occupy a distinguished academic chair in the national capital in the name of the great son of Karnataka, Abdul Nazir Sab. A one-time corpus fund will sustain the chair and its academic activities which will have a tremendous impact at the national and the State levels.

22

What We Can Do?

S.A. Ravindranath

I have become a minister after I served as a member and thereafter as the Chairman of my village Panchayat. That is why even now I visit Panchayats frequently. On such occasions the Chairmen of the Panchayats sit by my side. If something is wrong with the bore well, or if the drain is blocked, or something is wrong somewhere, these Chairmen sit as though they have no responsibility. They point at the legislators and ministers. But they should realize their responsibility. When we are trying to reach power to the grass roots, they can do a lot of good things at their level, within their limits, within their finances. But even if a nut has to be replaced in a bore well, many people are not ready to get it repaired through their secretary or the bill collector. This is my experience. Even now I stay in my village in Davangere. When in Bangalore I may stay in my ministerial bungalow, but whenever I go to my village I stay in the village. In order to learn what village people are doing, what they like, etc., I visit at least two or three villages on my tour.

Today the government is giving a lot of funds. Within the funds received we should do the best we can or do what is absolutely necessary. If the bore well has failed, we try to get it repaired through the Gram Panchayat or the Zilla Panchayat or the State government. I have seen small, minor problems. Since there are restrictions on spending money, in many villages which I have visited, the streets in the Harijan settlements can be made usable by putting a

V-shaped or U-shaped drain, or by doing a little gravel work. But that is not done. People cannot even walk on those streets. I have seen this in many villages.

Since I was the Chairman of the Panchayat I got done almost everything I could and now they have to only replace the bulbs or fuses. I did not do these things because I wanted to be a minister. I come from an ordinary peasant family and I have done whatever I could for my village. My feeling is that if you do whatever is possible in a proper way there will be no need for the State government.

When we were the Chairmen of the Panchayats we used to feel very happy to receive a grant of Rs. 5,000. Today you get nearly Rs. 5 lakh. In addition to this, in some places, if you do good work in schemes like the Employment Guarantee Scheme, etc., a situation will arise that when we come to your village you may as well say that you have nothing to ask of us. My desire is that the Panchayats should become self-reliant. You should all work in that direction.

I got urinals and toilets constructed in my village when I was the Chairman. Many people opposed it. But ultimately it is the village people who benefit from such things and no one else. Today they have stopped the construction of urinals and toilets. Apart from this, they are not cleaning the tanks and channels also.

In many towns the situation is the same as in our villages. Wherever necessary our government gives two lakh of rupees to construct community toilets. In addition to this, if toilets are constructed for all in the villages, the Central government gives an award of Rs. 4 lakh. Mostly it is the Panchayats in North and South Kanara that have bagged these awards. Elsewhere people ignore such things.

These days, there is a reservation of 33 per cent of seats for women in our Panchayats. Hence if toilets are constructed, it would be very good. It would be something that brings dignity. In addition, whoever is below the poverty line, he is being given Rs. 1,200 and we propose to increase this to Rs. 2,000. Along with this money, if we can also contribute something and carry out the works in a better way, it would be good. Because compared to other countries, the toilets in our country are few. Our women are forced to go to open places either after the sunset or before the daylight. This is a matter of shame in my view. Today wherever there is a woman President at least in such Panchayats toilets should be constructed for all the villagers. This is my request at this juncture. All of you should earn a good name. As a matter of fact I have not been able to get a good name as a minister which I did as the Chairman of the Panchayat. Because I did good work in my village I have become a minister today. But still my villagers call me as Chairman only. So to earn a good name you should also do good work in rural areas, you should do honest work. If something good has to happen to Karnataka it must first happen in the village Panchayats. Only then can our State make some progress.

23

Solve the Problems and Move Ahead

C.M. Udasi

You have participated in the discussion on the path traversed by the Panchayati Raj during the last 20 years. With a view to make rural development a success and to take the country on the path of progress the central government established a Panchayati Raj system for the entire country based on the Karnataka model. However, there are people who say that the two-tier system brought in earlier was a better system. Even so, the three-tier system has been made mandatory all over the country. With a view to see that the three tiers of Panchayati Raj succeed in bringing about the desired level of rural development, the elected Panchayat representatives of Karnataka have been invited to this convention. Others should learn about your experience and your views.

In the discussion that took place yesterday, you have raised many questions like reservation, rotation of reservation, whether the term of office of the Presidents and Vice Presidents of the Panchayats should be 20 months, 30 months or 5 years, etc. You must have thought in your minds as to why reservation is limited to you and not extended to the members of the legislative assemblies and the Parliament. You might have also thought that Udasi is contesting elections from the same constituency since 1983, but for us we don't know whether we will get another chance to contest elections from the same constituency or not. So far as the question of reservation for women is concerned, it started with 25 per cent and has now reached 33 per cent but actually their representation has touched 46 per cent.

Only yesterday some of you expressed the view that it would be better if women are given 50 per cent reservation. I also want to implement that policy if I get an opportunity.

We are thinking of introducing the Ombudsman system, if possible this year itself, to see that the money given to the Panchayats is utilized properly. When the Panchayats do wrong things, the Ombudsman will take action. The Ombudsman will oversee the working of the Panchayats, hear complaints about Panchayats and the departments that come under their jurisdictions and will bring about greater discipline. This has become inevitable.

Make Gram Sabhas Successful

More important is the fact that if the Panchayati Raj Institutions have to succeed then the Gram Sabhas should be held successfully. What did people like Mahatma Gandhi, S.K. Dey, Asoka Mehta or Abdul Nazir Sab who dreamt of Panchayati Raj system think? They thought that no injustice will be done to the villagers by the Gram Sabhas, and hence only works suggested by the Gram Sabhas should be undertaken and only then would it be possible to give people a transparent administration. But you are aware that so far the Gram Sabhas have failed, even in Karnataka. I wish to bring to your notice that it is only if the Gram Sabhas succeed then other development works will be successful. You must be knowing that in the SJRY scheme, the Gram Sabha has to give technical and administrative clearance to schemes costing Rs. one lakh or more. Gram Sabha's decision is final. But in how many Gram Sabhas has it been possible to do this? All this is within your knowledge. In future the SJRY scheme will be implemented in 11 districts.

Earlier, the National Employment Guarantee Scheme was implemented only in five districts. We are extending the scheme to six more districts. In all these six districts, the Gram Panchayats will have scope to do a lot of work. Earlier there was a restriction that a Gram Panchayat could implement the scheme only within its own limits. Now we have divided work between different tiers. From now onwards, when the Taluk Panchayats build roads in rural areas, they can utilize the Employment Guarantee Scheme. When the Zilla Panchayats are carrying out work on irrigation canals, they can utilize the scheme. Last year we were paying Rs. 62.50 per day per person as wages. From 1st April, 2007, the wage has been increased to Rs. 74. In all these districts, 90 per cent of the money for rural development comes from the Central Government and the State Government contributes 10 per cent. All this money must be utilized properly.

You have discussed many issues. The most important issue is the one of upgrading the post of the Secretary of the Gram Panchayats and their selection at the earliest. There is also a suggestion to have a Directorate of Panchayat Personnel. We have already set in motion the work of upgrading the post of secretaries of Gram Panchayats and their selection. I hope it will be done very soon. Some people said that some works are being done outside the jurisdiction of the Panchayats. Watershed works are being done outside the Panchayat jurisdiction. There is a demand that this type of work should be entrusted to the Panchayats. I will try to set right the issues that have been raised in today's discussion.

The Question of Tenure

We have entrusted the responsibility of providing drinking water to the Zilla Panchayats. They should set right the drinking water system. One of your demands is that the reservation should be rotated after ten years. That will require an amendment to the Act. In my opinion it is better to get the Presidents elected directly and then make their term five years. It we only extend their term to five years it will not serve any purpose. Some of you have given me a memorandum that the term of the Presidents should be extended to five years and that no no-confidence motion should be moved against them for three years. We can provide for barring the no-confidence motion. But what if the President himself resigns? We cannot prevent his resignation. People who make you the President, or those who give you this power, may themselves make you resign, or better still, they may make you the President after obtaining your resignation in advance. If this happens what is to be done? So, I feel that it is better to get the Presidents elected directly. I feel it would be advisable to implement this at the Gram Panchayat level and see the results before extending it to the other levels.

We have given you Rs. 4,907 crores. This is your money. You should know that this is tax payers' money. If this money is to be properly utilized, you should have a feeling that it is not the government's money but your own money. You should see to it that the money is not misspent. This morning people from one Panchayat came to me with a complaint. They said that the Panchayat President and Secretary together had drawn Rs. 5,11,272. The department came to know after six months that the money had not been used but eaten. We are getting thousands of complaints of this type. Though it is the responsibility of the Department to look into these complaints, you should also find out what was the income of the Panchayat during the year, how much grant was received from the government, how that grant was spent, etc., and discuss all this during the *Jamabandi* programme in the Gram Sabhas. If this is done on a continuous basis, I feel that these kinds of complaints will become rare. If you take special interest in these things as you work, the respect people have for you will increase.

Many younger people have got elected this time. When I contested the municipal elections in 1974, we could get only widows to contest for elections. This was the situation about 25-30 years ago. Only those who were above 50 or 60 years of age were becoming the members of the Panchayats. Today the situation has changed. Now married women and sometimes even unmarried girls are contesting elections. If 46 per cent of women are getting elected, that means 10 times that number are contesting. We see that many of them have not only interest in becoming Presidents but also have the capacity. Earlier it was difficult to find even one woman to become the President. You are all like me, like Ravindranath. We are former youth and you are future old people. By the time you reach our age you would have an opportunity to become a legislator or a Parliament member.

There was also a complaint that the officers are not attending the Gram Sabhas. We will issue necessary orders that they should compulsorily attend the Gram Sabhas. There is also a demand that the executive officers should be appointed only from the Rural Development and Panchayati Raj Department and not from other departments. There can be no two views on this. But appointments have to be made in the department. Once the appointments are made we will set this right.

Today, there is need to establish an International Centre for Panchayati Raj and other local bodies. There is also a demand for establishment of an Abdul Nazir Sab Chair in Delhi. I will discuss this with the concerned persons and take an appropriate decision. With this I conclude and thank you !

24

Way Forward

C. *Narayanaswamy*

Two decades have elapsed after the new Panchayati Raj system came into existence in Karnataka. The Institute of Social Sciences and the Department of Rural Development and Panchayati Raj have organized this two-day convention to take an overview of the ups and downs of the system in these two decades and to learn our lessons and to churn out ideas as to how to make them the institutions of local self-government in the true sense of the term.

The august presence of personalities like the Union Minister for Panchayati Raj, Mani Shankar Aiyar, the Rural Development and Panchayati Raj Minister of Government of Karnataka, C.M. Udasi, the Chairman of the State Finance Commission A.G. Kodagi, former Minister Leeladevi R. Prasad, Additional Chief Secretary and the Development Commissioner, Government of Karnataka, Falguni Rajkumar, the Principal Secretary, Rural Development and Panchayati Raj, Government of Karnataka, M.R. Sreenivasa Murthy, the Chairman of the Institute of Social Sciences and Jnanapith awardee U.R. Ananthamurthy and the Director of Institute of Social Sciences, George Mathew, at the inaugural function added grace to it.

Mani Shankar Aiyar has explained in detail and very convincingly how the Panchayati Raj system has taken two steps forward and one step backward, how Karnataka which was at the forefront of implementing the Panchayati Raj system in the entire country has now slipped from that position and what you, the elected representatives, should do to bring it back to its pristine position. C.M. Udasi has spoken about the purpose of this convention. Mrs. Leeladevi Prasad in her unique style has taken us back by twenty years to the time of Ramakrishna Hegde and Abdul Nazir Sab. Kodagi has given evidence of his sincerity in his speech.

There were five parallel sessions on important aspects of the Panchayati Raj system. In these sessions, prominent senior leaders, senior legislators, experts on Panchayati Raj system and the senior officers of the Rural Development and Panchayati Raj Department of Government of Karnataka participated. An interesting feature of the sessions was that the persons working as the Presidents and Vice Presidents of the Panchayati Raj institutions shared their experiences with enthusiasm with other representatives. In the afternoon, some persons who have, with innovative practices, tried to solve the common problems facing Panchayati Raj institutions, and succeeded in mobilizing resources and increasing efficiency in service delivery with the cooperation of the people, shared their experiences with the audience.

The Chief Minister was scheduled to participate in the concluding session of the convention. Udasi had personally explained the importance of the convention to him. The Chief Minister had also evinced great interest in attending the convention. You were also eagerly waiting for him to come so that you could submit your memorandum to him. But when it was known that the Chief Minister would not attend the function, there was some reaction on your part.

I have seen Udasi from close quarters for many years. I have seen how he works even when he was the Public Works Minister. After he assumed the responsibility of the Panchayati Raj Department, he has been honestly and sincerely trying to see that the Panchayati Raj institutions implement effectively the people oriented programmes, so that development may take place in the real sense of the term. We have to welcome his efforts. He took so much interest in this convention that when the proposal came, he directly called the Director of the Institute of Social Sciences at Delhi and obtained information about the convention and then directed his officers to see that the convention was a success. As a result of this it has been possible for us to organize the convention so well and for you to come from every nook and corner of the State in such large numbers and participate in the convention.

Dr. U.R. Ananthamurthy is the Chairman of the Institute of Social Sciences. The Institute has its headquarters in Delhi and has a branch office in Bangalore. George Mathew, the founder Director of the Institute is ably assisted by a team of dedicated workers. This institution has done many good things concerning decentralization of power, empowerment of women, the urban local bodies and environment not only in this country but also in other countries.

Karnataka Model is Still among the Best

To talk about Karnataka, in 1983 there was a new experiment in decentralization of power. The tireless efforts of Abdul Nazir Sab and the commitment and desire of the then Chief Minister Ramakrishna Hegde, brought the Zilla Parishads and Mandal Panchayats into existence. This experiment attracted the attention of many countries interested in decentralization all over the world. After the Constitution Amendment in 1993, the earlier Panchayati Raj law was replaced by a new law. In these two decades the system has seen many ups and downs.

Karnataka was a model for the entire nation, but as Mani Shankar Aiyar said yesterday, we still have to go a long way in that direction. A comparative study of the Panchayati Raj systems in different States should be possible. Though it appears that our system has many shortcomings, it also appears to have many commendable features compared to the systems existing in most other States including Kerala. We should not forget that we have some schemes, some systematic outlines about which we can be proud. Wherever we have slipped we have to set things right and forge ahead.

Many elders have participated in this convention. They have freely expressed their views. We have opportunities to take our Panchayati Raj system to the highest level in the country. We have to work in that direction.

When we say that the Panchayati Raj system that came into existence 20 years ago was revolutionary, we cannot forget Abdul Nazir Sab. He is always alive in our villages. To keep his memory fresh and permanent, the Institute of Social Sciences has suggested the establishment of a Chair in his name in the capital of the country. I hope the minister will give attention to the suggestion.

Every year the grants being released to the local bodies for development and various programmes are increasing. There is a proposal in the recent Budget to release more than Rs. 4,950 crore during the financial year 2007-2008. We have to appreciate this. In addition to this the government has taken steps to strengthen the Gram Panchayats which are nearest to the people. A higher percentage of grants is being given to the Gram Panchayats. The problem of shortage of staff appears prominent. This has to be looked into. We also have to look at the appointment and transfer, etc., of this staff. As there is a Public Service Commission at the centre and one at the State level also, there is need to have a Panchayati Raj Service Commission to look after the appointment of Panchayat staff and matters related to their service.

To ensure a higher level of people's participation in local governance, the Constitution and the Panchayati Raj Act give more importance to the Gram Sabhas. We have even gone further down and created Ward Sabhas at the constituency level of the Gram Panchayat members. It is a fact that these institutions have not been functioning properly in many areas. But the representatives here have said that in the light of the experiences recounted here it is possible to set these things right.

Though many parallel organizations, both government and non-government, have been working within the jurisdiction of the Gram Panchayats and acting as though they are not concerned with the Panchayat system. That these parallel organizations are involved in the development process which lies within the development jurisdiction of the Gram Panchayats is unfortunate. You should pay attention to this also. To protect the importance of the Panchayati Raj institutions we will have to strengthen them. You have to cooperate in this process.

You have actively participated in the convention, you have aired your problems and have given suggestions also. You have particularly demonstrated that a very good leadership has developed from the village level, from the grass roots level. Our sisters here have worked with dedication. I hope we will continue to work towards making these institutions successful.

25

A Memorable Event

M.R. Sreenivasa Murthy

When Ravindranath was the Chairman of a Panchayat, they were getting a grant of rupees 10 or 15 thousand. The tax they were collecting during those days was hardly a few hundred rupees and not thousands of rupees. He has said that during those days they strived to fulfil the needs of the villagers. It would be better if some of you can go to his village and study as to how they worked. He has said that he became a minister because he worked with dedication. You must ponder over these things because they are important.

Secondly, our Rural Development and Panchayati Raj Minister Udasi has said that he has studied only up to 7th or 8th standard. But how many people can we get today in politics who can speak and write like him in Kannada and English? He has gained this knowledge by continuous self-efforts. He is an example to show that in whatever field we may be, whether it be politics, administration or any other field, it is possible to gain knowledge through sustained efforts. I wish to humbly impress upon you that if these two examples, i.e., developing one's personality through sustained efforts and creating a better atmosphere in our villages by organizing and uniting the people, can be retained by our Panchayat representatives, who are mostly youngsters, not only will your future be bright but the entire rural situation will improve tremendously.

The minister said that we should construct toilets. There is a proposal to send one of our officers to Holland to get training in construction of toilets. Our officers are also ready to go. We are also ready to send them. What is the use of sending rockets in space and exploding atomic bombs and what is the use of the revolution in information technology, if we have to go to Europe to learn how to construct toilets? We have to ask this question to ourselves. They never construct the kind of toilets that we need. They spend thousands of dollars and construct posh bathrooms in their countries. We must learn how to construct toilets at very low costs. Can our Panchayats not do at least this one thing? The Government has announced that it will give limitless grants for this. Now the Central Government has given *Nirmal Gram Puraskar* award to 110 villages. We are sending 110 Gram Panchayat Presidents to Delhi. On April 17th, the President of India is giving these awards. In these 110 villages toilets have been constructed in each and every house.

We are giving Rs. 40 to 50 lakh to every village as grants. Kodagi may recommend that we must give more. His report is getting ready. But if within the funds available to you, if you can at least give this one facility to the villagers, would it not be possible for them to live a healthy life permanently? This is the third question which should remain in your minds. Before going back to your villages if you can keep some of these things in your mind, I feel something good can happen to your villages.

Our minister has come to participate in this convention gladly. He also desires that the Rural Development Department should be improved, the Panchayati Raj system should be strengthened. But everyone knows that the Panchayati Raj institutions at present are very weak. He is eager to make them strong. I wish to thank him also.

Kodagi is another example you must keep in mind. Earlier he was an MLA. He had also contested to the Zilla Panchayat and had worked as the Chairman of the Standing Committee on Education. He never considers any position as high or low. When I was talking to him for about half an hour today, I felt that if more and more people like him were in our midst, our Panchayati Raj system could have worked so well. He was saying, why is every one asking for more grants for himself? Let them ask for more grants to their Zilla Panchayats, for the Gram Panchayats. He was saying that this demand for more grants to themselves, whether by members of Parliament, or Assembly, or Panchayats or Municipalities, is a very strange demand. Even this man with a simple life style can be a good example for everyone in public life.

When I was working as the Chief Secretary in one Zilla Parishad, C. Narayanaswamy was the President in another Zilla Parishad. To tell you the truth, there was always competition between us. Because whatever the people in Bangalore did, the people in Mysore wanted to do in a better way. Whatever the people in Mysore did, the people in Bangalore wanted to do in a still better way. But because people in Bangalore were in Bangalore they were getting better publicity. Due to this healthy competition both the Zilla Parishads could earn a better name. In the same way, it was possible for many Zilla Panchayats like those in Dharwar or South Kanara districts to bring a good name to the system through such leadership. Because in this leadership there was less demand for power for themselves but there was more desire to develop their villages, their districts. We discussed such subjects extensively, but as far as I remember the question of more powers never came to be discussed. So you should also keep such examples in mind.

Dr. George Mathew and his colleagues in the Institute of Social Sciences and those friends who came voluntarily are mainly responsible for the success of this convention. The officers of our department also lent a helping hand in their efforts. They have worked day and night to see that you are not put to any inconvenience and have helped in conducting the discussions and debates. I thank all the office bearers of the Institute of Social Sciences, their friends and all the friends of our Department, and more than anyone else, I thank you for having come all the way here to attend this meeting; in spite of whatever inconveniences you may have had, you have participated in the discussions and made this convention a great success and a memorable event.

Parallel Sessions

Session I

People's Participation : Political Parties, Planning from Below and Gram Sabhas.

This session was presided over by Abdul Aziz, Visiting Professor, Institute for Social and Economic Change, Bangalore and Ashraful Hasan, Director, Rural Development and Panchayati Raj, Government of Karnataka, N. Shivanna, Associate Professor, Institute for Social and Economic Change, Bangalore, J.C. Madhuswamy, Member, Legislative Assembly, Karnataka, from Chikkanayakanahalli, Tumkur District, B.S. Hiremath, Director, (Gram Swaraj Project) Rural Development and Panchayati Raj, Government of Karnataka and Sunandamma, Member, Gram Panchayat, Hosur spoke in the session.

Ashraful Hasan expressed the view that Gram Sabhas are not being conducted properly. He felt that they should be conducted during April-May and October-November every year. All voters and the head of the school, the Medical Officer, the Animal Husbandry officer, Bank Managers, Anganawadi workers and all other officers should be invited to the Gram Sabhas. The Secretary should report the activities of the Gram Panchayat. All department officials should give information regarding their departmental activities. All proceedings of the Gram Sabhas should be recorded.

B.S.Hiremath said that poverty, unemployment and illiteracy are the main features of rural life. These problems have to be solved in the Gram Sabhas. Persons deprived of benefits should participate in the Sabhas. Local level planning can optimize service delivery to the rural people.

J.C. Madhuswami said that priorities should be fixed as required by the Gram Sabha. Then a blue print should be prepared. The country can progress only if planning is taken to the grass roots. We have to mobilise resources and build assets. We must plan keeping the next generation in mind.

Sunandamma said that even after 50 years of independence Gandhi's dream of Gram Swaraj has not been realized. Gram Sabhas are the roots of democracy. Women and oppressed people should be given sufficient opportunity in the Gram Sabhas to speak.

N. Shivanna spoke on the need to motivate people to attend the Gram Sabhas and provide them with complete information on Panchayat matters. They should be encouraged to ask questions.

In the discussion that followed Rajegowda of Chamarajnagar said that when an application is given for Ashraya house, nobody bothers. Ravikumar of Maddur asked how they can create assets without sufficient resources. Smt. Yashoda said they are not given facilities to improve villages. Kumaraswamy from Hassan said that there was a shortage of engineers.

Session II

How effective is financial autonomy?

This session was presided over by Manu M. Kulkarni, Honorary Senior Fellow, Institute of Social Sciences, Delhi and A.G. Kodagi, Chairman, State Finance Commission, Government of Karnataka, Devendra Babu, Assistant Professor, Institute for Social and Economic Change, Bangalore, K.K. Patnaik, Former Director, Department of

Panchayati Raj, Government of Orissa, and Yashodamma, Member, Zilla Panchayat, Kolar were present in the Session.

A.G. Kodagi said that every Gram Panchayat should exercise the powers of a government. If the Panchayats have to become self-sufficient, they must give priority to mobilizing their own resources. Every panchayat representative should behave with responsibility and should have commitment. They should act in accordance with the Constitution. He wanted party politics to be kept away from the Panchayati Raj institutions.

Yashodamma disclosed that when the district plan for 2006-07 was read out to the Zilla Panchayat members, nobody understood anything. This should not happen again and members need to be trained in these matters. Money is not being given to some Taluks. When the cabinet decides to extend some facilities to some villages directly, where is the need for Panchayats? Zilla Panchayats do not have power to tax. How far is it advisable to have Gram Sabhas simultaneously in 7 to 8 villages, she asked?

Devendra Babu said that there should be four kinds of decentralization. Political decentralization to take decisions, administrative decentralization to control personnel, functional decentralization to provide services to the people and fiscal decentralization to mobilize resources.

K.K. Patnaik reminded the Panchayat representatives that they should not always look to the State Government but become self-reliant by mobilising their own resources.

Then followed a discussion in which John D'Souza of South Kanara, T.G. Manjunath of Bangalore Rural District, Sudha Shiva Bhatt from North Kanara, etc., participated.

Session III

Administrative Reforms : Can we have District Governments, and Why Parallel Bodies?

This session was presided over by Araga Jnanendra, Member, Legislative Assembly, Karnataka, Teerthahalli,

Shimoga District; D.R. Patil, Member, Legislative Assembly, Karnataka, Gadag; Sharanaprakash Patil, Member, Legislative Assembly, Karnataka, Sedam, Gulbarga District; T.R. Raghunandan, Joint Secretary to Government of India, Panchayati Raj, New Delhi; and Lalitha Chandrasekhar, Sociologist, Bangalore, spoke in the Session.

D.R. Patil explained the rationale for decentralization of administration and said that the villages were carrying on many administrative functions like running the Anganwadis, etc., smoothly. He exhorted the elected representatives to forget their political differences and work together.

Sharanaprakash Patil felt that changes were needed in line with modern development methods. Experienced officers should be brought to the district level. Planning is very essential for the development of rural areas and local leaders should be empowered to conduct the planning exercise. He said that we don't need a law to carry out programmes for the welfare of the people.

T.R. Raghunandan spoke on how it was not possible to bring about democratic decentralization between 1983 and 1987. Today Kerala stands first in implementation of the Panchayati Raj system and Karnataka stands second with Sikkim as the third. But Maharashtra and Tamil Nadu have got the most 'Nirmal Gram' awards.

The panchayat institutions lack resources and hence they should be provided with enough funds. Sikkim is doing well because the State Government gives Rs. 20 lakh to each Gram Panchayat there. Though women are given 33 per cent reservation in Panchayati Raj institutions they constitute only 2 per cent in the administration, that too only in Uttar Pradesh.

Lalitha Chandrasekhar recommended that opportunities be provided to students to participate in the Panchayati Raj institutions. She said that it is unfortunate that no serious discussions take place in the Zilla Panchayats. Much discussion centres on drinking water and housing.

Even though grants are given they do not reach the Gram Panchayats.

Araga Jnanendra said that along with decentralization of power, corruption has also been decentralized.

Session IV

Women and Weaker Sections in Panchayati Raj : Role of Judiciary, NGOs and Media

This session was presided over by Motamma, former Minister, Government of Karnataka; Shobha Karandlaje, Member, Legislative Council, Karnataka; N.J. Usha Rao, Director, National Institute for Integrated Development, Bangalore; Suman Kolhar, Facilitator; Singamma Shrinivasan Foundation, Bangalore; Kalasamma, Member, Gram Panchayat, Naganahalli, spoke in the Session.

Kalasamma, welcomed the participants and detailed the problems faced by gram panchayat members. She said that women members do not have training before hand and that the members belonging to the backward classes are treated badly. She also said that proper information is not given in the Gram Sabhas. She demanded that women be given 50 per cent reservation.

Shobha Karandlaje, said that the Scheduled Castes and Tribes are making some progress because of the reservations provided to them. However, the Presidents are themselves taking advantage of all the developmental works. Gram Panchayat members should protest against injustice and exploitation.

Motamma observed that the meeting showed that women have become emboldened after training and the media is also showing appreciation. They are now participating in meetings and conferences with courage. Women members of the Panchayats should boldly ask for the copies of the circulars issued by the Government. Women members are treated well only till their signatures are obtained and later they are ignored. They should sign only after reading the documents and understanding the implications. She mentioned that recently 2,000 women in Gejjalagere village of Chamarajnagar District were trained to drive tractors.

N.J. Usha Rao said that women should participate in all struggles. They should not feel inferior because they are not educated but should try to become literate and send their daughters to schools. She further cautioned that NGOs should work honestly.

Suman Kolhar wanted reservation to be extended to two terms as in Tamil Nadu.

In the discussion that followed Pratibha of Samaj Parivartana Kendra said that though women can speak on any subject they confine themselves to merely signing on the dotted lines. Suvarna of Sulya Taluk, Dakshina Kannada district said they do not have any money to provide drinking water and they are facing difficulties in collecting taxes.

Session V

Good Governance, Accountability and Nyaya Panchayats

This session was presided over by V.K. Nataraj, Former Director, Madras Institute of Development Studies, while Vishweshwara Hegde Kageri, Member, Legislative Assembly, Ankola, District Uttara Kannada; Ashokananda, Director, Abdul Nazir Sab State Institute of Rural Development, Mysore; Buddhadeb Ghosh, Former Director, State Institute of Rural Development, Kalyani, West Bengal; and Shilpa. P., Member, Gram Panchayat, Horatti, spoke in the Session.

Vishweshwar Hegde Kageri, opined that the secretaries of the panchayats were mainly responsible for the deterioration of the Panchayati Raj system. We should ourselves take on the responsibilities and work.

Buddhadeb Ghosh said that if the Panchayats have to become successful there should be proper dissemination of information. Panchayats should act responsibly and be answerable to the people. They should respond to the aspirations of the people but act only within the framework of law.

Shilpa. P. stressed participation in Gram Sabhas and unity among the people. She said that for the last two years, they are imposing fines on people who do wrong things.

Ashokanand said that we should respect democratic values. There should be at least one meeting of the Gram Panchayat in a month. We should respect each other. He also mentioned that corruption was creeping into the Panchayati Raj system.

V.K. Nataraj expressed the need to amend the Panchayati Raj Act to bring it in consonance with the 73rd Amendment of the Constitution, like the West Bengal Panchayati Raj Act.

In the discussion that followed, Gayatri Devi, from the Institute for Social and Economic Change asked whether the panchayat members have introspected about themselves? Phalakshappa, member of Gram Panchayat from Davangere said that every Gram Panchayat should have an engineer. There is shortage of secretaries. Secretaries do not have correct information. Mutturaj, President of Gram Panchayat from Mysore District complained that officers do not come to Gram Sabhas. Shailaja, former Vice President of Bangarpet Taluk Panchayat in Kolar District said that the Ration Cards were not being distributed properly.

Index